World War Two - Annandale Connections

Isabelle C Gow

*This book is dedicated to my family
and the people of Annandale.*

INTRODUCTION

Annandale is situated in the centre of Dumfriesshire in South West Scotland. The River Annan, giving its name to the valley, rises in the Moffat Hills and flows into the Solway Firth near Annan.

The route through Annandale bringing trade and travellers from the north and south to the border is an ancient one and nowadays is still the main gateway to England via the M74 and the West coast railway line.

It is a quiet rural area, with a green rolling landscape which is the setting for medieval castles and the Georgian and Victorian estates and mansion houses of several border families.

Two of Annandale's most famous sons are King Robert the Bruce whose family had castles at Annan and Lochmaben and the writer, Thomas Carlyle, who was born in Ecclefechan.

During the Second World War, Annandale became a hub of activity due to the huge number of military personnel; civilian workers; prisoners of war; convalescing servicemen and evacuated children coming into the area. After the war ended many of these folk remained and made their homes in Annandale.

This book attempts to tell some of their stories.

FOREWORD AND ACKNOWLEDGEMENTS

It has been a real privilege to meet and talk to so many brave men and women and their families. They told me their stories and entrusted me with their precious photographs. They advised me to speak to others and provided me with contacts so that over the 18 months I gradually built up a huge network of new friends. I just hope that this book will do justice to their remarkable stories.

I know there are more stories – every person who lived through those dark times has a tale to tell and I apologise to those folk whom I never got the chance to interview or the villages I failed to visit. This book can only be the "tip of the iceberg."

With thanks to:

The Staff of the following establishments:- Lockerbie Library, Ewart Library (Dumfries), Dumfries Aviation Museum, Annan Museum, The Devil's Porridge Exhibition, Lockerbie British Legion, Hallmuir POW Camp, Solway Offset the Printers.

Tony Walker ex- Barony Agricultural College, Professor Tony Hellen (POW Camps), Agnes Dougan of Wishaw (Lanarkshire Yeomanry), Lesley Aitken (access to Johnstonebridge Primary School logbooks), Graham Herbert (access to Lockerbie Academy Admissions Registers), Dr Jack Wilson (Lochmaben Town Council Minutes) and Michael Hurst MBE, director, Taiwan POW Camps Memorial Society.

Finally many thanks to those whom I interviewed and those who provided me with contacts, memories, stories and photographs:-
Lord Annandale, Margaret Barbour, Ann Bell-Irving, Malcolm Bell - MacDonald, Elizabeth Blacklock, Jim Blackstock, Maria Bojanitz, Jean Bowyer, Betty Campbell, Eileen Campbell, Isa Carruthers, McEwan Charlish, Irene Clark, Bill Clement, Matt Cochrane, Sadie Cockburn, Ronnie Cunningham-Jardine, Lou Crolla, Michael de Luca Jnr, Michael de Luca Snr, Emilio Dicerbo, Billy Duncan, Isabel Fogg, Jack Gaster, Bill Gibson, Eileen Gordon, Jack Graham, Jimmy and Annie Graham, Bella Grant, Alan and Mary Hannah, Douglas Hannah, Dave Henderson, Ian Henderson, Annie Herrick, Peter and Hannah Hills, Bill Hunter, Chrissie Irving, Jock and Madge Jardine, Mattha Johnstone, Peggy Kacedan, Gordon Kerr, Raymond Kirkbride, John Knipe, Sir David Knox, Lorna and Charlie Lamb, Mr & Mrs Tom Laurie, Jack and Isobel Maxwell, Jean McCauley, Hannah Moffat, Dora Mundell, Margaret Nairn, Jim Neill, Jean Patterson, Dorothy Reetz, David Richardson, Janette Richardson, Mary Ritchie, Marjory Ross, Paul Roxburgh, Davy Shankland, Alec Smith, Andrew Spence, Sarah Steele, Drew and Grace Taylor, Eric and Nan Till, Jim and Wilma Twidale, Eric Watson, Morag Williams, Elsie Wilson, Jack Wilson, John and Ann Wilson, Violet Wilson, Duncan Wright, Bob and Daisy Young.

My apologies to anyone I may have inadvertently missed.

CONTENTS

Chapter 1
The Men in the Forces

From 1939 men, the length and breadth of the country, were either enlisted or conscripted into all the different branches of the armed forces. What follows are personal memories and relatives' stories of a small percentage of these men, who either were from or now live in Annandale, who helped win the war for the Allies. Some recount remarkable feats of bravery; some remember how they defeated fate; some recall their involvement in the most crucial and momentous events of the war and some tell of the non-combatant tasks they carried out which allowed their comrades to continue fighting.

Army – **The Lanarkshire Yeomanry; Andrew Gibson; Ned Carruthers; The McNaught Brothers; Peter Hills; Bill Clement; Jim Campbell; Jim Twidale; Michael De Luca; Hector Shennan.**

Navy – **Davy Shankland; Albert Lamb; Duncan Wright; Billy Richardson; Gilbert Henderson; Mattha Johnstone; Jack Gaster; Jack Wilson**

Air Force – **Eric Till; Matt Cochrane; Ian Henderson; Hugh Dowding**

The Italian Resistance – **Michele De Luca**

The Lanarkshire Yeomanry

Several local men belonged to the Lanarkshire Yeomanry which had squadrons based in Lanarkshire and Lockerbie. This was a volunteer cavalry Territorial Regiment which suited country lads who knew how to ride and indeed they had to provide their own horses. At the outbreak of World War Two, the Royal Artillery Field Regiments, the 155th and 156th, were formed from the Yeomanry and also conscripted men. The 156th were deployed in Europe and the 155th in the Far East against the Japanese. Many of the 155th were taken as prisoners of war in Malaya after the fall of Singapore in February 1942.

Sgt. Andrew Gibson from Thorniethwaite Farm, Lochmaben was called up and took his pony with him - it was called Marlake and used to run at the point to point. Andrew was posted to Malaya but he became ill and was taken to hospital in Africa just before many of his regiment were captured. Sadly Andrew never recovered from TB.

Many ex POWs have written accounts of their time spent as prisoners of the Japanese. Also a short film about the Lanarkshire Yeomanry was made recently by South Lanarkshire Voluntary Television and posted on their web page and **Agnes Dougan**, the daughter of an ex - POW from Wishaw, along with a group of others, are recording a history of the regiment.

Andrew Gibson

One of their members was the late **Jim Watson** who was born in Moffat. Jim had spent three and a half years in Japanese prison camps - first Changi and then in Taiwan where he was forced to work in the copper mines at Kinkaseki. His book "Memoirs" tells the story of the appalling conditions endured by the men there. Remarkably, Jim survived for more than 60 years after his release from this camp that had reduced him from 12st 4lbs in 1942 to 7st in1945.

The story of **Jock Wyllie** and his life as a Japanese POW is told in a later chapter.

Archibald Carruthers
KOSB
"A Bridge Too Far"

Ned Carruthers

Archibald A Carruthers, otherwise known as Ned, was born at Corrie Common near Lockerbie. After school he worked on a local farm and then at 17 began to work for the Castlemilk Estate. With several other workers he decided to join the Territorial Army reservists and in September 1939 enlisted with the King's Own Scottish Borderers.

After training at St Boswells he was soon off to Europe and eventually found himself at Arnhem, the battle made famous by the film, "A Bridge Too Far". Unfortunately, Arnhem was a disaster, but Ned survived having two close shaves with bombs failing to explode next to him. He managed to escape to safety over the River Rhine on a raft.

This was not the only time he visited Arnhem. Shortly after the war had ended, the army was looking for volunteers to help with the exhumation of bodies at the battle site. These bodies were to be reburied with full battle honours in a dedicated cemetery. Ned volunteered and discovered that the battle site was also a film set. The film, called "Theirs is the Glory"- a much more accurate account of the war than the more famous "A Bridge Too Far"- needed extras for the battle scenes. Ned was once more in the thick of fighting!

Ned also spent some time as a member of the Allied forces imposing the surrender terms on the Germans in Norway.

Once demobbed, Ned returned to the Castlemilk Estate from where he retired in the 1980s. Ned had married **Isa McNaught** from Palnackie in 1946. They lived at Corrie, raising their family and contributing much to the local community and church.

Isa's story is told later in this book.

Ned Carruthers (still from film)

Arnhem Cemetery in Netherlands.

The McNaught Brothers

Ken McNaught

KOSB Badge

I spoke to **Isa McNaught** about her husband **Archibald Carruthers** and discovered that Isa's three brothers and she herself also played important roles in the war.

The family originated from Palnackie in Kirkcudbrightshire. **Robert Kenneth (Ken) McNaught** worked on a farm and later as an artificial inseminator in Hightae. When he was 18 he was called up and joined the KOSBs as a fusilier. He saw time in Burma and survived the war, but unfortunately died very young.

Black Watch Badge

His brother, **James Wallace McNaught (Wall)** also began army life with the KOSBs and then fought in Africa with the Black Watch. He was wounded and hospitalised, but survived the war only to also die very young in a coal mine accident.

Wall McNaught

The third brother, **Herbert (Heb) Kitchener McNaught** was exempt from the army as he was a farm worker at Jardine Hall Main Farm, but he joined the Home Guard.

Peter Hills
Black Watch
Cook
Lockerbie resident and member of the British Legion

Peter Hills

Peter was born in 1926 at Bexley Heath, Kent. At age 17 Peter volunteered to join the Royal West Kent Home Guard as he wanted to avoid becoming a Bevin Boy. The following year after D Day he was called up for the Black Watch and his first posting was to Cameron Barracks in Inverness, then to Perth then to Milkbank at Lockerbie.

Peter was a cook and got sixpence extra in his pay for this.

He used to make up the haversack rations - hard boiled eggs - for the battalion training. They would train for a week under canvas on the Langholm circuit. He told me that the men knew that if their name was drawn to leave on a Wednesday they would be going to France, if it was a Saturday then they would be off to the Far East.

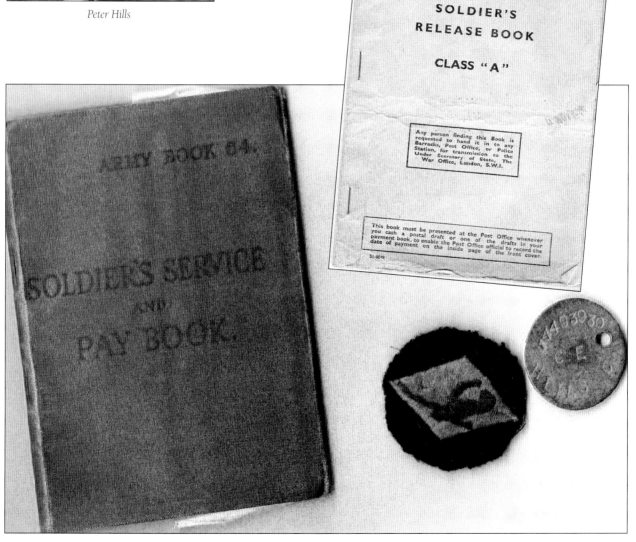

Bill Clement
Black Watch Piper

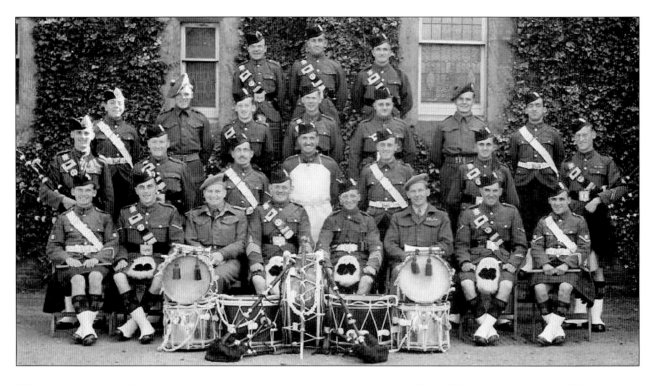

Bill was born in Perthshire, but spent several months as a piper in the Black Watch stationed at Milkbank near Kettleholm. At 3pm every Saturday, Bill and the other members of the pipe band played for the crowds whilst marching up and down Lockerbie High Street.

Called up in 1942, Bill, joined the Black Watch and after basic training was sent to Barrow-in-Furness for embarcation leave. The day before he was due to sail for North Africa, he was told that he would only go if so and so failed to turn up, otherwise Bill was to report to the Pipe Major. It turned out that Bill never did travel to Africa despite having his tropical kit at the ready.

Bill had been an apprentice joiner when he left school and was keen to carry on his studies in order to go to university. He started a correspondence course and when he was sent to Milkbank the army allowed him one day per week to carry on with his studies if there was a suitable venue. The headmaster of Lockerbie Academy, Johnstone - Hetherington, was known to Bill's family and so with his

help Bill found himself not only working on the correspondence course but also spending time in the technical department with the woodwork teacher, Mr Williamson. Much later after the war Bill qualified as a technical teacher and taught at Wallace Hall in Thornhill.

Bill recalls his time at Milkbank with great affection. He and the other piper, Alex McRae, got to know many local farmers and townspeople. After the "Beating of the Retreat" every Saturday in Lockerbie they were both invited up to Mr and Mrs D K Wilson (the bakers) to have afternoon tea. On Sunday evenings they went to Mainhill Farm, south of Lockerbie, to enjoy a farm meal and to play cards (solo whist) with Mr and Mrs McBride. There were also a son and two daughters who were all very musical. Bobby played the fiddle; Martha the accordion and Elsie was the pianist.

Bill takes up his story:- "The Brigade Sports were held in Kettleholm with other regiments taking part; the Seaforths and the Argylls. It was unfortunately a dreadful day of rain. The piping judge was Pipe Major Willie Ross. He just sat inside a bell tent while we piped in front of him in the rain. Alex McRae got first place in the March competition and I got first in the Strathspeys and Reels.

The piper's Nissan hut, where we slept, had tables, covered with a blanket, at one end of the hut. It was round this table where we did our chanter practice, learning new tunes. A stove stood in the middle of the hut which we appreciated in the winter, and many evenings we made toast and occasionally scrambled egg (powdered egg). One very cold day in October, we had the stove on while we were at our chanter practice. Unfortunately we had a visit from our Company Sergeant Major who said that fires in barrack rooms were not permitted until a date later in the month. Now that I had been appointed Lance Corporal Piper, I was consequently placed on a charge and would have to appear before our Company Commander the following morning. It was fortunate that I had to visit the tailors' workshop that afternoon where I noticed they had a fire in their stove, so enquiring how they managed this, I was told that was because it was their workshop. Next morning armed with this information, I paraded at our Company Office. When the charge was read out and I was asked for an explanation I said that our hut served two purposes: one as a barrack room and secondly as the pipers' workshop. I was then told by our Company CO it was possible to have a fire during practice times, but the Sgt Major was furious.

One of the tasks of the pipers was to pipe on route marches for those soldiers still on training. On one of these marches Alex and I marched 33 miles. Each tune we played ten or more times then, after a short break, still marching, we started another tune. All day we never repeated a tune. From Kettleholm we made for Tundergarth and Bankshill, then on by Puddockhole, after which we headed north for Boreland, eventually wading the Drfye Water. Our 33 miles ended at a farm where the platoon was to spend the night in a barn. A truck was there for Alex

and I to travel back to Kettleholm. We were asked to play a tune by the farmer and his wife. Of course we were happy to oblige and played several selections, but just before we finished piping, a wasp entered my mouth as I took a breath and stung me on the lower lip. The two of us were invited into the farmhouse for tea, where there was a wonderful spread on the table and I could not eat a thing!

This was a two day march for the platoon in training although the pipers returned to camp at the end of day one. There was a three day march known as the Langholm circuit which included Longtown and Langholm. Although I do not have a clear memory of this I do recall piping through these two towns.

The battalion had a good relationship with the Lockerbie folk and before we left to move north, D K Wilson, on behalf of the council and the people of Lockerbie, presented a drum major's mace to the Pipe Band President, Major John McGregor as a thank you."

By the age of 23 Bill was a Pipe Major and nowadays he still teaches piping!

Presentation of the Mace.

Jim Campbell
Royal Armed Artillery

Jim Campbell

Jim Campbell's family farmed at Todhillwood near Canonbie. When war broke out he was too young to join up so joined the Canonbie Home Guard where he remained until 1943. He was then called up as part of the Royal Armed Artillery Corps a section of which was the 11th Hussars. With the Hussars Jim trained in the UK including some time spent under canvas at Wentworth Golf Course in preparation for the D-Day landings.

Jim sailed over to France from Newhaven on the third day. He'd never been abroad before and spent most of the crossing seasick. He landed at King's Beach which was part of "Gold" Beach where armoured cars were waiting.

Trooper Campbell belonged to a reconnaissance group for the 7th Armoured Division. They headed for Rouen, stopping now and again when they came across the Germans. When they reached their destination their officer ordered the men to climb up the church steeple to see what was around them. Jim was the driver and he stayed in the car with the officer. He thought he should brew up a cup of tea so he got it ready along with the tinned pudding that was intended to be their "cake". The officer advised that he go inside the church to tell the men that tea was ready rather than shout. However, the Germans had sighted them; the corporal was coming down one side and Jim going up the other with bullets flying all around and whizzing by them, but unfortunately for Jim one went through his foot. So much for the tea, Jim was invalided out firstly to a field hospital and then flown back to the UK. He still has the bullet in his possession.

His foot was badly infected and took several months to heal. Jim spent the rest of the war being transferred from one hospital to another. He remembers being cared for at Jardine Hall for a short period and being entertained there by ENSA.

Jim returned home safely, but sadly his brother, John, was killed in the fighting in Western Europe.

Trooper Campbell

Jim Twidale
Royal Engineers
Corporal

Jim Twidale

Jim Twidale was born in Grimsby and as a young lad had been a runner for the fire service. He enlisted in the army in January 1945 and was first sent to Inverness and then ended up in Lochmaben Railway Station one dreich night at 9pm from where he was taken to Halleaths and given damp straw to fill a palliasse. Not very welcoming, but Jim remained in Lochmaben after his demob and married **Wilma Harkness** from the burgh.

Jim was in command of some POWs who had been brought to Halleaths Army Camp and he remembers one incident very well concerning a German POW known as "the Architect". One of the prisoners' tasks was to march on foot from Halleaths to the Kirk Loch to paint and oil a bailey bridge, but one dreary, misty morning one of the POWs refused - he said he couldn't go out there; he was an architect. Jim couldn't have his authority challenged and ordered him through the interpreter, a German called Harry, "Out - or I'll be forced to shoot!" The man went into hysterics so Jim told Harry to take him by the scruff of the neck and the seat of his pants and kick him up the backside; put the brush in his hand and tell him to get on with it. The interpreter told Jim that he was pleased to do that because this "architect" was a Nazi. Jim had to make enquiries about this, but promised Harry that he wouldn't say who had given him the information.

When they returned to camp, Jim discovered that he had to report to the major and tell him the story. Jim was told that it was just as well he hadn't used his gun. At 9pm a sergeant and 2 corporals came for Jim to get ready to go to Edinburgh to be interviewed. There at HQ a captain asked Jim how he knew the man was a German officer, but Jim would not tell as he'd given his word to the interpreter. He only said that by the man's general manner, his ability to speak English and not being used to taking orders, he thought that he might be an officer. Jim found out later that he was also a relation of Krupps, the arms' dealers. The man had taken an identity disc from a dead German. (If he'd been discovered to be a Nazi he would have been sent to a much more secure camp.)

The captain still demanded that Jim tell him his source of information but Jim had given his word that he would protect Harry. He was told that he would be charged and he was interviewed for five hours. When Jim got back to Halleaths he told the major how he had been treated. The major phoned Scottish Command and told the captain that Jim was owed an apology. At the time there was another man at Halleaths whom Jim thought to be an officer. He was right then too. This POW was a major in the German army.

Jim Twidale

Jim couldn't tell this story until now because of the Official Secrets Act.

Army Transport

The De Luca Family

Michael De Luca of Lockerbie forwarded me this story of his father and grandfather's war. It is one of both serendipity and of extreme bravery.

"There are an estimated 70-100,000 Italian Scots living in Scotland today, almost 2% of the population. Many, like the De Luca family emigrated to Scotland in the 1890s to escape poverty and famine. The family originated from Atina, a town south of Rome and north of Monte Cassino, and like many other Italian families at the time found their niche in ice-cream and fish and chip businesses throughout Scotland.

Michael and his brother, **Jimmy De Luca** were both born in Lockerbie – 'above the café', but at an early age they were taken to Italy for their education and so they could learn more about their parents'country of birth. The family home was a house appropriately named 'Villa Lockerbie' on the outskirts of Atina where they ran a small farm and vineyard. The house is still owned by one of Michael's sisters.

Villa Lockerbie

A few days before the outbreak of World War 2, Michael set out with his father, **Michele**, to return to Scotland to join Jimmy, who was working in the family business in Lockerbie. However, they were stopped at the Swiss border and because Michele had an Italian passport he was not allowed through. Since young Michael had a British passport his father gave him a choice – return to Atina with him or continue alone to Scotland. He chose to go on. The reason? So he could smoke on the train journey without his father knowing. He was 14 at the time, the cigarettes were Craven As!

On returning to Lockerbie Michael helped with the fish and chip business at the back of the café as well as playing the piano accordion with his brother, Jimmy at the Rex Cinema in Lockerbie – a gig that earned them free cinema tickets for years.

When they were old enough both Michael and Jimmy were called up for service in the British Army. Jimmy in the Pioneer Corps and Michael in the KOSBs.

Michael and Jimmy De Luca

Michael embarked for the D - Day invasion of Normandy, but was only in France for a short time before being wounded in the leg and shipped home. Before this he and some of his fellow KOSBs were involved in a narrow escape in Bayeux. While there, Michael had spotted an accordion in a music shop and decided to buy it – a strange thing to do in a battle zone. The troops were billeted on a farm and one day the queue in the washroom was so long Michael suggested they get the accordion out and play a few tunes. His mates left the queue and followed him over to the trenches. Just then the farm came under attack from mortar fire and the farmhouse was totally destroyed. If they had stayed in the queue, the chances are they would all have been killed.

Meanwhile in Italy the Gestapo had commandeered Villa Lockerbie as its headquarters in the area. Michael's mother and sisters had to leave the house and were taken in by the family of Charles Forte. It was not quite so comfortable for his

Michael De Luca

This certificate is awarded to

as a token of gratitude for and appreciation of the help given to the Sailors, Soldiers and Airmen of the British Commonwealth of Nations, which enabled them to escape from, or evade capture by the enemy.

H.R. Alexander

Field Marshal,
Supreme Allied Commander,
Mediterranean Theatre

1939-1945

father, Michele, however, who took to the hills with some of the local men and formed a resistance group. As an English speaker he was able to pass on valuable information to the Allies. Michele did not speak much of his time in the Resistance and in fact most of the next generation knew nothing about it until his grandson Michael found a certificate in the attic of the café and started asking questions about it. It was awarded to Michele by Field Marshall Alexander, Supreme Commander of the Mediterranean Theatre for bravery in helping the Allied servicemen evade capture and escape the enemy.

After the war the family were reunited in Lockerbie although frequent visits have been made to the house in Atina.

The De Luca family have now been in Lockerbie for four generations and Michael's grandson Vincent still has a business there today."

Michele de Luca

Atina devastated in WW2

Hector Shennan
RASC
at Dunkirk

Hector and Flora Shennan

The evacuation of Dunkirk was one of the low points of World War Two, but for the soldiers who managed to make their way back to the UK they were met with great rejoicing. It is a remarkable story of human endeavour. Every boat that was seaworthy was put into commission to bring back the tired and weary soldiers.

My grandfather, **Hector Shennan**, was one of the local men who was brought back to safety. Unfortunately he was badly affected by his experiences and was invalided out of the army, only to die at the age of 43 of peritonitis at home in 1944.

In the Annandale Herald and Record of July 4th 1940, a local, **unnamed soldier** wrote about his experience of Dunkirk.

"The immense pall of smoke from the blazing oil well and the gaunt outline of shattered buildings gave this town an unreal appearance. We spent four days in Dunkirk - four days rendered horrible by the incessant air raids. The whine of the bombs and the ensuing explosions, coupled with the bark of defending guns, was unpleasant. Due to the constant need for taking cover the whole party got split up, and I spent my last evening in Dunkirk with four others in a cellar near the docks. The night was rendered horrible by delayed action bombs exploding. Along with us in the cellar were a number of French civilians, many of them old people and little kiddies. The courage that those poor people displayed was wonderful; in spite of all they had suffered they remained cheerful. Dawn brought with it a spectacle of utter destruction. Debris from shattered buildings was strewn broadcast, tangled telephone wires, burnt- out vehicles and bomb craters were everywhere...

I decided to try to get out into the country and find some means of reaching the coast at a quieter spot...En route I picked up three other fellows who like myself were lost. Several miles further on we found the road blocked by heavy French artillery and streams of refugees and French mounted troops converging on Dunkirk. Turning back we headed for the Belgian frontier and spent the greater part of the day dodging enemy planes. Eventually we reached Nieuport where we found Nazi planes heavily bombing the town and had to turn back. A few miles back along the same road we were forced to make an abrupt halt and dive frantically for cover as an enemy plane dived down upon us. As we reached safety a bomb exploded, and no more could be seen of our vehicle except twisted and smoking ruins. After various minor experiences we arrived at La Panne and ultimately embarked upon a destroyer.

We were astonished to see lines of craft of every description passing us, their crews cheering and waving. It was the Merchant Navy going to rescue those who were left, and a grand inspiring sight."

Hector Shennan

Davy Shankland, MBE
Leading Signalman
Royal Navy

Davy Shankland

Davy is a well known face in Lochmaben and thereabouts - a keen fisherman and enthusiastic Burns' speaker, he worked for many years at Lochmaben Sanatorium as a nurse and later as a nurse tutor, having been the first male nurse to train at Dumfries Infirmary. It was a wartime event, however, which led to Davy choosing nursing as a career.

Davy was born in Kirtlebridge and when he left school he worked in Annan in the printer's office. Davy decided to enlist in the Royal Navy at the end of 1942 when he was only 17.

His first ship was the HMS Royal Arthur and his first posting was to South Africa, but en route he was redirected to the HMS El Hind. (This had been a merchant ship commandeered by the navy when war broke out.) Most of Davy's three and a half years' service was in the Far East and in 1944 he was aboard this ship in Bombay (Mumbai) harbour while it was awaiting a refit as it was due to take part in the D Day landings.

On 14th April 1944 Davy had the morning watch. Through his telescope he saw the arrival of the Fort Stikine. Little did he know then that this ship would change his life.

At 8am Davy handed over the watch and went below deck. Everyone was in good spirits as they were looking forward to the return voyage to Britain. After lunch, Davy decided to take a siesta, but it was cut short when around 4pm he was awakened by loud voices shouting that the Fort Stikine was ablaze in the harbour.

Davy went to get a better view and fortunately for him he was sheltered by the bulkhead when the Stikine exploded. Flying metal and fires everywhere made it seem as if all hell had broken loose. Davy's first instinct

The El Hind

was to jump overboard, but the sea was burning because of all the oil, which had leaked from ships.

Soon afterwards another explosion caused a huge tidal wave in the harbour, but this at least put out the fires on Davy's ship.

The El Hind drifted out off the harbour and Davy began a head count - only 6 others were alive. 243 men were killed, but Davy wasn't so sure that he and his companions would survive. All seven men were tired, hungry and emotionally drained, however help did appear.

A small boat was sighted – a LCP (landing craft personnel). Davy dived over and swam to the craft. Luckily he was able to get the engine started. Soon he was alongside the El Hind and his companions were able to get on board. After about 15 minutes, the El Hind exploded and sank to the bottom of the sea.

Davy and his six crewmates landed safely and were rushed to hospital.

At the time the Government did not issue an official announcement about the Bombay disaster, however a local enquiry in Delhi discovered that the Fort Stikine had been illegally carrying a mixed cargo of raw cotton and 700 tons of bombs. The enquiry reported that 14 ships had been sunk and an estimated 3000 people killed. Ironically hardly any of the crew of the Fort Stikine had been killed as they had been on shore leave.

Davy recalled that it was really very difficult for him to adjust to civilian life after having experienced this tragedy. I suppose today the diagnosis would have been post- traumatic stress. He felt guilty for having survived.

In order to expiate this guilt, Davy decided not to return to his printing job, but do something, which would help people. He enrolled as a student nurse at Lochmaben Sanatorium in 1946. In 1953 he was accepted for training and by 1961 he had enrolled at Edinburgh University to study to be a nurse tutor. His dissertation was "The Role of Male Nurses".

Davy worked in several local hospitals until his retiral in 1989, his lust for life having returned many years ago. He was awarded an MBE in 1984. Davy is proud of this, but he finds greater satisfaction in knowing that he has trained countless men and women to become good nurses.

Davy Shankland front left.

Albert Lamb
Gunner
Maritime Royal Artillery

Albert Lamb

Albert was born in Lochmaben in 1911. After leaving school he served his apprenticeship as a baker.

When war broke out, Albert volunteered for the artillery as he was keen on shooting. As a gunner he travelled the world visiting Canada, Buenos Aires, Africa and the Mediterranean.

Malta, a strategic position in the Mediterranean, had been heavily bombed (154 days of continual bombardment) and desperately needed supplies of foodstuffs as well as oil. Previous convoys had been unsuccessful and by August 1942 the people were starving. The War Cabinet proposed Operation Pedestal and the men and boats were to be carefully selected for their experience in the Atlantic convoys. This became known as the Malta Convoy and included Albert.

The oil tanker involved was the American SS Ohio. When it sailed into the Clyde it took on British registration and a British crew. To protect its precious cargo, guns were bolted down on the

Albert's Medals

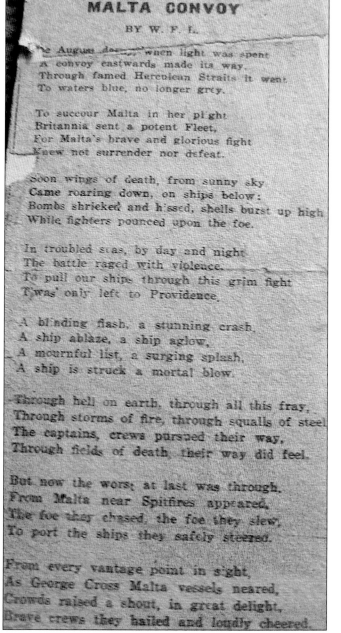

Poem written about the operation

HMS Ledbury Survivors   (Wikipedia)

deck, and this was where Albert was needed. The convoy was the most heavily bombed in the war and only five out of the fourteen merchant ships survived, despite being protected by cruisers, destroyers, aircraft carriers and battleships. The Ohio was attacked on all sides by both German and Italian planes. It lay in a critical position when the HMS Ledbury appeared to fight off an attack by German Junkers, however Ledbury was again called away to pick up survivors from another ship. By then the destroyer Penn had come to the rescue to tow the tanker into the harbour. Twice the tanker had to be abandoned by the crew, but finally with the aid of the Ledbury, which had returned, and the Rye and the Braham, the sinking ship eventually entered the harbour and Malta was saved from surrender.

The captain, Dudley Mason, was awarded the George Cross for his efforts. So important was this operation and so famous that there were even poems written about the Malta Convoy.

As a souvenir, Albert had brought home a Maltese flag which the family recently returned to Malta as a piece of memorabilia for its museum.

Albert received 5 medals including the Africa, Italy and Atlantic stars.

When Albert returned to Lochmaben, he married a Dumfries girl, Janet Maxwell and raised a family there. He was part of the team which constructed Chapelcross and then later worked for Bluey Wells and then ICI. Once retired Albert, enjoyed a simple game of dominoes on a Thursday night. Who would think he'd led such a dangerous early life?

Duncan Wright
First Class Stoker
Royal Navy

Duncan Wright

Duncan was born in 1924 at the Bogle Hole, (Marjoriebanks), Lochmaben and was educated wholly at the local school. He worked for McMichael's the bakers, first as a delivery man with horse and van and later with a motorised van.

When Duncan was old enough he first served in the Home Guard as a "general flunkey". He recalled that they met in the Town Hall in Lochmaben where Adam Smith was a stickler for drill and getting them off their mark - "Home Guard was right up Queen Street before you could get them turned."

Duncan told me a story about his friend, Jock Milligan who was a corporal in the Home Guard. Jock was on manoeuvres at the "Bogs" (M' Banks) near the wood. He was told to go into the wood to "check for German paratroopers" and report to the captain Jim McGhie. He saluted and said "The Germans are in the wood; the cushies are fleeing oot," (cushies = pigeons) "And while we are at it, what about the subsistence for my bike? I just work at Corncockle Quarry, not own it!"

When Duncan was 18 he was called up for the services and was asked what he did for a living. As a result he was given the job as a motor mechanic in the coastal force and from there went on the motor gun boats - the MGB605. Men were only allowed to serve on them for 6 months as the vibrations from the huge American Packard engines could damage their backs. His next posting was on the aircraft carrier Formidable. He saw 3-4 years of service and fought at Okinanwa, known as the Japanese Gibraltar. The Formidable also provided cover for the bombardment of Kuri Harbour.

Towards the end of the war the Formidable sailed from the Admiralty Islands picking up ex - servicemen and Australians who'd been in Japanese POW camps and took them to Sydney. Then the ship returned to the same camp to transport Indian POWs back to Bombay. Duncan's ship brought home a large number of Kettleholm boys who had been POWs. Duncan was pleased that he was able to write to Mrs Dalgleish (near Hightae) about

The Formidable

Kamikaze Wreckage – from Duncan's photo album

Wull Green

Duncan Wright (centre)

her son, Georgie who had been taken prisoner by the Japanese, and tell her he was alive - her first news of him in years.

Duncan told me about an acquaintance, Sam Clegg, who'd been on the MGB605 with him. He met him again

Boiler Damage

at Portsmouth and asked him what he was doing there. Sam had been on a 605 whose bows had been blown off by a German destroyer and had returned from the Dutch coast in reverse gears!

Another well known Lochmaben man, Duncan's half brother, Wull Green served in France with the Royal Engineers.

Billy Richardson
Able Seaman
Royal Navy

Billy's sister, Peggy, said that Billy went away a boy and came back a man. She didn't know him. He was born in 1924 and before he was 18 he was up at Prestwick helping to build the airport. Then he was called up in 1943 and chose the Royal Navy. He saw service on two boats - the Onyx - and the Ledbury which was a minesweeper in the Mediterranean. Often he was at sea for months, but he was lucky and survived the war.

Their cousins, John and Ian Richardson, were also in the navy. They never met up with each other during the war, but they all survived.

Billy Richardson

Billy on the Onyx

Gilbert Henderson
Able Seaman
Royal Navy

Gilbert Henderson worked in the agricultural industry before he joined the navy. He served mainly on the battleship HMS Nelson which witnessed some of the most significant events of the war.

During 1943-44 Gilbert was on board HMS Nelson as it supported the invasion of Sicily which led up to the Italian Armistice. This was signed by Eisenhower and Marshal Badoglio on board the Nelson. After a refit the Nelson then played a part in the Normandy Invasion, but was struck by mines. She was sent to Philadelphia for repair after which she was deployed around Ceylon for a few months. At Penang the Japanese forces formally surrendered aboard the Nelson!

Gilbert Henderson

The Nelson *(Wikipedia)*

Mattha Johnstone
Royal Marines

Mattha was called up at the age of 20 and sent down to Kent for training before posting abroad. In June 1943 he was a dry land marine working as a torpedo engineer for the Mediterranean operations at the time of the invasion of Sicily. He stayed in the Marines until 1953. He recalled that every day was an adventure; he was young and not too worried.

Mattha told me about another Lochmaben able seaman: **"Duke" Paterson** who served on the Penelope, the Furious and the Cleopatra. The Penelope was torpedoed near Anzio and sank in 1944; the Furious took part in the attack against the Tirpitz in 1944 and the Cleopatra served in the Mediterranean and afterwards was the first ship to sail into the recaptured base of Singapore in 1945.

Jack Gaster
Sub Lieutenant
Royal Naval Commandos

Jack Gaster came to Lochmaben 16 years ago. He appreciates the quiet peace of the burgh – after all he had survived the D-Day Landings.

In 1942 Jack was employed as an apprentice in a tug boat and kept busy carting the bomb rubble down the Thames in London. He had volunteered for the Royal Navy several times, but was told he was in a reserved occupation. Some time later Jack heard that volunteers were required to man the lighters (barges) which were being converted into landing craft. This time he was accepted as Seaman SCO with a huge salary of 15/- a day! These men were nicknamed " The Millionaire Mob".

After initial training, Jack set off for the Isle of Wight to learn how to handle the landing barges and the machine guns as well as learn Naval signalling. When his contract ended, he was given several career choices. Jack decided to stay on with the flotiila as an instructor. In 1943 Jack sat his exams, passed and was promoted to Sub. Lieutenant RNVR. He was drafted on to HMS Armadillo, which was a commando - training base on Loch Long. After 10 hard weeks he became Assistant Beach Master and posted to RNBC 'J' Commando (Royal Naval Beach Commando).

Jack in uniform whites - Singapore 1946

At the beginning of February 1944 Jack was training in earnest for the invasion of Europe. His job would be a dangerous one – first off the craft and onto the beach to check it was the correct one, mark the area out for the others and set up the beach signals. He was there on 6th June on "Jig Beach, Item Green" at Le Hamel near Arromanches (Gold Beach). They met a fair bit of opposition, but not nearly as bad a reception as the Americans received at Omaha Beach. There was a big cliff along the front, however, and plenty of Germans on the top of it. The beach had been mined and the men under fire.

Jack recalls that he had a "body guard" to protect him while he was regulating the beach and checking for mines. Meanwhile the materials that were to be used to build the Mulberry Harbour had safely arrived. Jack remained on the beach until 23rd August when the Allies had broken through to Caen and the commandos were no longer needed.

One incident he remembered was watching at very close quarters a Petty Officer dismantle a mine. Everyone else had fled!

When Jack left France he had his first British meal in the Waverley Hotel in Edinburgh. They entered the dining room still in their uniforms, but were politely asked to remove their revolvers – they were so used to them they had forgotten where they were!

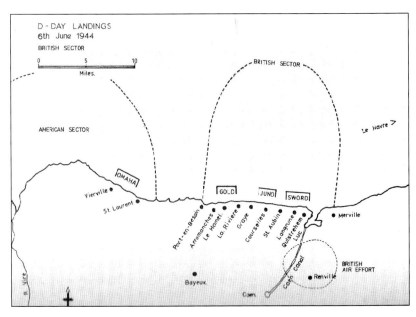

Map Showing D-Day Landings

Dr Jack Wilson
Surgeon- Lieutenant
RNVR

Lochmaben resident, local historian and retired family doctor, Jack Wilson, spent two and a half years in the Royal Navy. First of all on "Saladin" - a small destroyer - on anti- submarine duties, escorting convoys from Milford Haven to Southampton and then on large landing ships in the Indian Ocean where he was present at the surrender of Rangoon, Singapore and the Andama Islands.

Jack graduated from Edinburgh University in 1943, but not until 1952 did he arrive at Lochmaben. During his time there, he saw many changes in medical practice with the introduction of many new antibiotics, improvement in surgical techniques and in diagnosis. Since his retirement in 1985, these changes have advanced further making medical practice even more complicated and he is in no doubt that his generation of GPs experienced the best years of the National Health Service.

Dr Wilson is a founder member of the Annandale Sailing Club and on retirement he bought an E boat (built for off shore racing) which he sailed at Kippford.

One of his other passions is history and he has published several booklets and books on the history of the Burgh of Lochmaben, as well as having transcribed "The Lochmaben Court and Council and Court Book 1612 to 1721".

The Saladin   (Wikipedia)

Flight Sergeant Eric Till
Flight Engineer
RAF

I met up with Eric Till who now lives in Lochmaben. I'd been at school with his son and daughter, but I had no idea what Eric's wartime experiences were. He has documented his own 'story' and has contributed to publications written by the Dumfries and Galloway branch of the Aircrew Association.

Eric was born in Annan, but was educated partly in India and Egypt as his father was a regimental sergeant major in a cavalry regiment, however the family returned to Dumfriesshire when his father was discharged from the army. Once Eric left school he became an apprentice engine fitter and when war broke out he served in the A.T.C. and the Home Guard until he was old enough to volunteer for the services. He particularly wanted to serve on motor torpedo boats in the Royal Navy, but after several months Eric had never heard from the recruitment services so he went along to the Naval Centre in Dumfries where he was told that he had not been called up as he was in a reserved occupation since his firm was training army fitters. Eric was not to be put off. He volunteered for the RAF and in due course Eric was enlisted and began training as a flight engineer.

At Cirencester he gained some experience of flying in Oxfords and Ansons before being sent to Newquay in the winter of 1943/4. Another three months were spent near Weston-Super-Mare, learning theory, electrics, more maths, first aid etc. Next came Technical Training on Halifax bombers and then more study followed by the award of his sergeant's stripes. Eric remembers once on leave he was walking along the platform at Cardiff Railway Station with two other newly promoted NCOs. They heard a policeman call out, "Sergeants!" It took them all a few moments to realise that the policeman was addressing them!

Next Eric was posted to Tilstock to join a crew. They were to become a tight knit team, however with a different crew Eric remembers a "sticky moment". He was mid flight when there was an undercarriage failure and Eric got thrown about the plane. Fearing the worst when he realised that there was a sticky fluid running down his leg he was mightily relieved to discover that the origin of the fluid was two squashed oranges!

His crew then learned how to tow gliders and soon went on to squadron training dropping paratroopers, supplies and jeeps for the French Resistance. Shortly after VE Day the squadron was actively engaged ferrying the airborne division of the K.O.S.B. to Norway and then flights to Brussels to return with freed POWs.

The war in the Far East had not yet ended and on the 18th July 1945 Eric and his crew took off for India. One of their tasks was to drop supplies of rice down to the starving people of Burma. In August Eric flew in the first Halifax plane to land in China and brought back POWs.

Once demobbed, Eric returned to his former job, but later entered the dairy business for a short time. However, he was to find his most challenging and rewarding work at Chapelcross Nuclear Power Station - on the site of a wartime airfield!

He kept his links with the RAF, being a member of the Royal Observer Corps; becoming a squadron leader of the ATC; and with his membership of the Aircrew Association. After several years' research, Eric was able to track down the other members of his crew and celebrate a reunion in 1988.

Eric in India (l-r no. 6)

Below are the two photographs of the crew - in 1945 and again in 1988.

Back row, left - right, Donald White, Eric Till, Bill Jones and in front Bob Crompton, Ray Smith and Eddie Ball.

Matthew Cochrane, DFM
Warrant Officer
RAF

Matthew Cochrane is a well kent face in Annandale:- he used to work as a salesman for the seed merchants, John Brown who traded out from the store (now flats) on Bridge Street, Lockerbie. The company then merged with SAI and Matt found himself often sitting in farm kitchens sampling the home - made scones while taking orders for seeds from the farmer.

Matt, himself, comes from a farming background. His father farmed at Catlins, outside Lockerbie, and when war broke out Matt volunteered, but was refused as he was in a reserved occupation so he joined the Home Guard. He was, however, desperate to join the air force so when the form came in the following year, he described himself as an "agricultural student". He joined the RAF in 1940, but he did not expect that three out of the six years he would serve, would be in training.

He was sent first to a signals recruiting centre at Blackpool where he learned Morse Code and some "square bashing", then on to Wiltshire for training as a wireless operator. This job would entail sending out his plane's position to the base every half hour in order to let the control know that they were still airborne.

Blenheim   *(Wikipedia)*

Another course on the Isle of Man saw him flying disused Blenheims. He also had to get used to the small single engine Proctors - just the pilot and him - while learning how to get in touch with the base. Next he was sent to Barrow-in-Furness on a gunnery course flying in Defiants.

After this successful training he was promoted to Sergeant and sent to an Operational Training Unit where he was teamed up with a pilot and navigator, engineer and gunner - five in a crew - on Wellingtons. At the end of that course the crew was sent to drop leaflets over occupied France. (These would be propaganda pamphlets encouraging the French resistance against the Germans.) Matt remembers one incident when his navigator made a mistake and they ended up flying frighteningly through the barrage balloons at Southampton!

Beverley in Yorkshire was his next base and it was there that he met his future wife, Joyce, who lived on a farm right next door to the runway. From there he and the crew (all Australians) flew out over La Rochelle and St Nazaire laying magnetic mines. Their pilot then volunteered the crew for Pathfinder duties based in Huntingdonshire. This was a crucial task because their plane would have to go ahead of the main bombers and light

Wellington   *(Wikipedia)*

up the targets by dropping a half load of coloured markers along with a half load of bombs. This was really dangerous and yet Matthew eventually did 56 of these missions. On the side of the plane they had painted a Kangaroo holding a bomb and so after every mission they added another bomb. (Matt's pilot accomplished 72 missions until he was shot down. He managed to parachute out, but was taken prisoner.)

Matthew told me about a raid shortly after D-Day. German anti aircraft guns were firing shells and one struck just below the plane making one of the engines pack up. The engineer was told to switch off that engine, but in his panic he switched off the intact engine! Luckily he was able to get it started again and they made an emergency landing as the pilot wasn't sure whether the tyres had been damaged. Once landed Matt found a piece of shrapnel under his seat and in the body of the aircraft there were about 90 holes! The only injury was that of the engineer who lost the tip of an elbow. In retrospect Matthew reckoned that that was the worst mission, but considers himself extremely lucky as on average 40 planes out of 80 or 90 on a raid would not return.

Matt Cochrane

After the cessation of bombing raids, Matthew asked to be transferred to Transport Command. This time he flew with 6 other crew members on converted bombers then Yorks. These were single missions flying our equipment and perhaps 30 or so troops at a time to places such as Tripoli, Libya, Palestine, Iraq, Karachi, Calcutta and Poona. Matt had a close shave when he and nine other men were trapped in a converted Stirling Bomber which crash landed - luckily for them - onto a sandbank. They managed to smash their way out through the astrodome. If it had hit anything else there would have been sparks and the plane would have exploded as there was petrol all over the floor.

Matt was actually in India when the war finally ended in August 1945 and it was there, he recalls bumping unexpectedly into his (now) neighbour solicitor, **Ian Henderson** who was serving as a RAF navigator.

Matthew was demobbed in 1946, having reached the rank of Warrant Officer and he was awarded the Distinguished Flying Medal. This was reported in the Annandale Herald: "For having completed numerous operations against the enemy in the course of which he has invariably displayed the utmost fortitude, courage and devotion to duty."

Distringuished Flying Medal
(Wikipedia)

Dropping leflets from a plane   *(Wikipedia)*

Ian Henderson DFM
Flying Officer
RAF

When war broke out Ian Henderson from Lockerbie was about to study law at Edinburgh University, but when he reached the age of 20 in 1942 he joined the RAF. He spent the first few months training in England, Ireland and Canada and then was based in Lincolnshire at Scampton. He became a navigator in Bomber Command with Squadron 153. The men are pictured here along with their ground crew. Ian is second on the left. The pilot was South African, Donald Legg; the gunners were a Scot, Jock Beat and an Englishman, Andy Andrews; the engineer from Largs was Jack Ross; the Bomb Aimer from Liverpool was a Welshman, Dave Jones, and the wireless operator - Russell Rawlings was from Canada. They discovered, after the war, that the pilot had bad eyesight and had memorised the reading charts in order to get through the eye test! That, said Ian, was the explanation of some "odd landings". They were lucky; remaining together and all surviving the 30 missions they flew in their Lancaster (P for Peter) Bomber. (See appendix 2)

Ian Henderson 2nd left and his air and ground crew

One of Ian's missions was the bombing of Dresden which was at the request of the Russians who believed the Germans were about to mount a counter attack. The orders to Bomber crews were to attack only military installations, but unfortunately there were strong winds that evening which led to the firestorm which destroyed so much of that city.

Ian Henderson

By this time the Germans had introduced the V2s and were working on an atom bomb. There seemed to be no clear indication when the war would end and Ian believes that the devastation that was Dresden probably had a psychological effect which resulted in the war ending sooner.

After the war in Europe ended Ian came back to Crosby near Brampton to train for longer flights over the Pacific Ocean. He was then transferred to Transport Command and posted to Karachi where he worked as a briefing navigator. The war in the East ended and so he was demobbed.

Elizabeth Thomson

He returned to his Law degree did further training and came back to be a solicitor in his father's law firm in Lockerbie.

He met his wife, **Elizabeth Thomson** (from Annan), at a dance in Lockerbie after the war. Elizabeth had been in the WAAFs working as a plotter, but was never posted abroad.

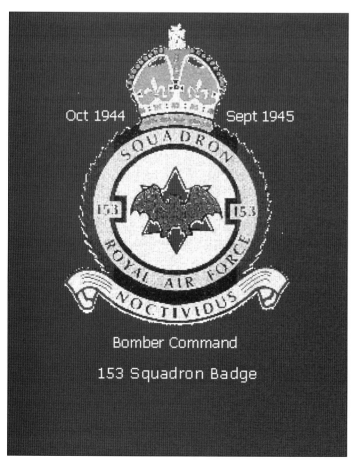

Badge of 153 Squadron

(Wikipedia)

Damage in London done by German V2 rocket

(Wikipedia)

Sir Hugh C T Dowding
Air Chief Marshal
RAF

One of the best known heroes of World War Two was born in Moffat in Annandale.

Hugh Dowding was born in 1882 in the house, where his father was a schoolmaster (St Ninian's), and which now bears his name as a sheltered home. The family left Moffat in 1897 for England and Hugh attended Winchester School. Afterwards, he saw service in the army and later in the Royal Flying Corps in World War One.

In the 1930s when he was Air Member for Supply and Research he urged the Government to develop new fighter aircraft (Spitfires and Hurricanes) and gave his full support to the research done by Robert Watson-Watt which would result in the creation of radar. When he became Commander-in-Chief of Fighter Command in 1936 he advocated improvements in all areas of air defence including airfields and internal communications.

He was a man of considerable foresight and imagination and perhaps underestimated in his day, however, he is now recognised as one of the masterminds of the Battle of Britain. Winston Churchill had referred to his leadership as "an act of genius in the art of war".

He reached the rank of Air Chief Marshal and was granted the title First Baron of Bentley Priory G.C.B., G.C.V.O.,C.M.G. The bronze and sandstone memorial to him in Moffat gives him the accolade: Leader of "The Few" Battle of Britain 1940 and Architect of Deliverance.

Above the plaque are Churchill's famous words " Never in the field of human conflict was so much owed by so many to so few."

CHAPTER 2
PRISONERS OF GERMANY AND JAPAN

While searching through back copies of the Annandale Herald Newspaper I came across several references to local lads who had been captured and taken as prisoners of war. These are but a few. [The Prisoner of War Camps in Germany mentioned below are Stalag VIIIB, Stalag X1B and Stalag XXA. V111B was near Lamsdorf (now Lambinowice) in Silesia; X1B at Fallingbostel in Germany and XXA was at Thorn (Torun), Poland.]

Privates Martin, Mundell, Baxter, Johnstone

In May 1942 the Annandale Herald reported that: "Mrs Baxter of Vendaceburn, Lochmaben had received a photograph from her son, Pte. Robert Baxter, from Stalag VIII B camp, Germany. He served with the KOSBs and is a prisoner of war. In the photograph are three other local men:- Pte. Robert Martin, Bridgemuir, Pte. Johnstone, Walnut Grove; and Pte. John Mundell, The Heck. Mr Martin was employed by Mr Beattie on his farm. Mr Mundell worked at Priestdykes Farm before the war and Mr Baxter was employed by Jardines, Painters and Decorators, Lockerbie. They had been taken prisoner in 1940." The photograph, however, was not printed.

Local Prisoners of War (Annandale Herald & Record)

Also in Stalag VIII B was Pte. **Douglas Bell Jardine**, 2nd Battalion Seaforth Highlanders, a native of Lockerbie. Before joining the army in1938 he was employed by Mr A W Wright, butcher, Station Road. (Private Jardine is in the centre of the front row.)

Lance Corporal Cameron
ROAC

Also in 1942 Mr and Mrs R Cameron of 87 Park Place, Lockerbie had received a photo from Stalag XXA (50) of their youngest son, Lance Corporal Dickson Cameron, of the RAOC and three other prisoners of war. "Prior to joining up he was employed as an electrician with Messrs Irving and McKinnon, Lockerbie. He was taken prisoner in June 1940 at St. Valery, France."

Corporal Cameron returned home in April 1945. He had been sent to Thorn in Poland where he had been set to work on a farm. "The farmer was a German who had taken over this farm from the Poles. The hours of work were long and the rations limited. In January because of the advancing Russian army the Germans evacuated the camp and forced the men to march towards Germany for about 12 weeks. The winter was severe and many nights were spent outside. From Cameron's column only 400 from the 700 who started completed the trek. At Soltan in Germany, Cameron and an Edinburgh man decided to escape. They got away and remained in hiding until the allies came."

His story is told in the Annandale Herald and Record. He also talked about his experiences in Poland and described how harshly the Germans treated the other nationalities particularly the Jews and Russians. He reported that the first and last six months were the worst because many of the Red Cross packages were not always distributed to them. When they were they were most appreciated. They also received sports equipment, but because so many of the prisoners were weak they could not make best use of it.

Company Sergeant – Major W J Little
KOSB

Local Prisoners of War (Annandale Herald & Record)

"A Moffat soldier, Company Sgt-Major W J Little of the 1st 5th KOSB who has been reported missing for some time, is now reported, through unofficial sources, to be a prisoner of war in France, though badly wounded. He is a keen Territorial, and on the outbreak of war was called to the colours and crossed to France with the Expeditionary Force. He is the son of Mr W J Little, baker, Well Street, Moffat, and well known in territorial circles."

Officers

Oflag 79 near Brunswick in Germany was home to three Lockerbie officers for about three years - **Lieutenant-Colonel W D Marshall, Lieutenant Alfred J Sillitto and Major V W S Leatherdale.**

"**Capt. J R Armstrong- MacDonnell**, the East Surrey Regiment, son of Mr W H A MacDonnell, Broomlands, Beattock who was previously reported missing, is now officially a prisoner of war."

Many of the local men who were prisoners in Germany were home by the end of May 1945.

Private James Johnstone
Gordon Highlanders

The Dumfries Standard announced in April 1945 that, "Private James Johnstone, a native of Ecclefechan, has returned home fit and well after spending nearly 5 years in a German POW camp. Enlisted in the Gordon Highlanders in 1939 and taken prisoner with the 51st Division at St Valery in June 1940, he escaped from a prison camp and returned with a number of other prisoners freed by the Russians from Odessa. As soon as he arrived home he was entertained in the public hall."

Lance-Corporal Ronnie
REME

The Annandale Herald and Record reported the return of Lance-Corporal John Ronnie, R.E.M.E.

Ronnie, a Lochmaben soldier, had been a POW for nearly 5 years. He had been captured at St Omer in France on 23rd May 1940. At that time he had received burns and was attended for five weeks by French doctors at Le Toquet where he had been taken by the Germans. Once judged to be fit he had to walk from Le Toquet across the north of France, through Belgium and into Holland where he was taken on board a barge. After 5 days he was then put into a cattle truck and transported to Poland. There were 55 men in the truck and they remained there for 2 days and a night. Their rations for the journey were three quarters of a loaf and a sausage. By the time they had reached Poland, many of the men were suffering from dysentery and had to be carried onto wagons.

Once they reached their destination the men were in better shape and settled down in the camp which had been adapted from an old fort. The daily ration was one fifth of a loaf, and a litre of soup. Occasionally some margarine and sausage was added.

John registered as a carpenter and was able to earn a little money to supplement the rations, but this did not last long. Those who wanted to work had to queue about 3am. By this time around Xmas 1940 Red Cross parcels began to appear and made a huge difference to well being, health and morale.

As a POW in Stalag XXA in Germany, John had written to his friends in Dumfriesshire via the Annandale Herald and Record in February 1942. He thanked the Red Cross and wished all his family and friends his best wishes. He gave thanks for letters and contributions and also indicated that he had met Dickson Cameron from Lockerbie and they had "a talk on the beauties of Mid-Annandale."

Rifleman Inglis

"Rifleman Thomas G Inglis, King's Own Rifle Corps, youngest son of Mr David G Inglis and the late Mrs Inglis of 12 Victoria Park, Lockerbie, returned after spending three and a half years in a German pow camp. Thomas was captured in North Africa by Rommel's Panzer division on 24th January 1942. He had been taken first to Sicily and then to a camp near Graima in Italy. He remained there fifteen months where he was joined by another Lockerbie lad, Pte. Edward Davidson of the Durham Light Infantry. Mr Davidson is the son of Mr and Mrs James Davidson of Whitecastles, Lockerbie.

When Italy was invaded, Rifleman Inglis was transferred by the Germans to the Sudetenland and for nearly two years he worked in a coal mine. His camp was liberated by the Russians on VE Day and ten days later the Americans took all the prisoners in the camp (1500 in all) by motor to Pilsen , Czechoslovakia." After a few days he was then sent to Brussels then home.

Privates Davidson and Carruthers

The end of May saw a welcome home party for POWs from Corrie. "Ptes Eddie Davidson and Willie Carruthers had spent time in a German camp. Pte Davidson had been captured in June 1942 in North Africa and Pte. Carruthers was one of the gallant band of KOSBs who held out until overwhelmed by superior numbers and lack of ammunitions in the bid for Arnhem. The hall was decked with flags and streamers, flowers and lots of home made food. There was music and gifts of cigarettes for the men. They all had a gran' nicht!"

Private Johnston

"Returning to his home at 6 Ferguson Place, Lockerbie in April 1945 was Pte. W A Boyd Johnston of the 2nd Queen's Own Cameron Highlanders. He had been taken prisoner at Tobruk on 20th June 1942 by Italians and sent to italy. After the Italian armistice he spent about 4 months trying to reach British lines, but he was recaptured and taken to Germany. He spent a few months in a camp near Berlin, then was transferred to Stalag X1B near Hanover where he was put to work in an oil refinery. Until Xmas 1944 conditions were not too bad, but later food was in short supply and largely consisted of potatoes only. By then the Red Cross parcels were stopped and mail had also stopped. In April 1945 the camp was liberated by the Highland Light Infantry. Before the war he was employed as a slater by McKinnon's of Lockerbie and later Gibson's of Lochmaben."

Private David Hodge
RAOC

"Liberated from a POW camp in Singapore in 1945 was Pte. David B Hodge of the Royal Army Ordinance Corps. He joined up in February 1941; left the Clyde in December 1941 as part of a large troop convoy and arrived in February 1942 in Singapore. 27 Japanese bombers attacked them on arrival and sank several ships including the "Empress of Asia'. David was ten days on the island then he was taken along with the other British and Australian servicemen to the camp where he spent 3 and a half years. He lived mainly on rice with a greenleaf stew, some Red Cross supplies, bananas and coconuts.

David was employed as an auctioneer and manager of Lockerbie Auction Market for Messrs Harrison and Hetherington."

David Hodge
(Annandale Herald & Record)

Private Sam Slaven
KOSB

Sam Slaven
(Annandale Herald & Record)

Sam's daughter, Isabel Fogg wrote to tell me about her father's experience as a POW in Germany.

"Samuel Slaven was born in a 'rural house', in an area outside Dumfries called Brownrigg, on 27th July 1919. His dad was called Frank and was known as 'Wattie', his mum, Jean Stephenson. Both parents were born in Ayrshire. Several of Sam's siblings joined the forces: Alec was in the south of England with the Royal Engineers; Charlie worked on the railway during the war; Francis was a RAF sergeant in the war and went to the Middle East; Jean was in the army and Mary was also in the army in Singapore.

As a child Sam moved several times as his parents looked for work. He remembers living outside Dumfries in Ruthwell and at Cumrue near Lochmaben. In 1936 he joined the territorials and was called to sign up on the Saturday before the Sunday on which war was declared. Davey Edwards went to the saw mills to get him to report to Lockerbie Drill Hall. At breakfast in the territorials there were ten men to a table and Sam ran 5 miles every morning. On one occasion he arrived back late and his ration of butter had been taken. This resulted in a fight which Sam won.

Sam was in the Kings Own Scottish Borders (KOSB), number 3188348, joining up in 1936. He landed at St Malo on 13th June 1940 and was captured on 18th June at Carentan, surviving an ambush which involved his truck being mortared and set alight. He remembers being lined up around a field 5 yards apart from the next prisoner convinced that he was about to be shot, as shootings and torture were happening all around. He was imprisoned at the 'Belle Vue barracks at St Lo spending some time at hospital with dysentery. When he returned to the Barracks his comrades had gone and he took on the identity of a Frenchman.

With no prior warning Sam was loaded into a crowded cattle truck and locked in for 3 days. He remembers using a corner of the truck as a toilet and the noise of the uncoupling of the carriages on their arrival at Stalag 4B, which was a massive camp, they were still fitting barbed wire to the tops of the fences when he arrived. Monsieur L'Abbe was a prisoner there too. They were counted at regular intervals in groups of five, however the lines at the back used to run to the left or right so that numbers did not tally. His stay there did not last long as his Frenchman's hat went missing. When he was shouted at for not having it whilst on parade, he could not answer appropriately. Questioning followed after which he was sent to Stalag 8B.

Stalag 8B was at Lamsdorf. His number there was 7901 and he arrived in 1941. Sam remembers no 'palliasses' but sleeping on straw on a cement floor. There was a huge stove that remained unlit, the men would sit around it 'warming their hands'. Sam was kept in a billet which was single storey with three rows of bunks from floor to ceiling. He described how prisoners would collect lice and sprinkle them on the Nazis' heads as they walked past. He walked behind a Nazi with a bayonet over his shoulder and managed to pierce a piece of paper on it, the soldier was blazing when he found it! Men were organised into working parties, at first he was put in the cookhouse with Jimmy Harraps from Edinburgh. He would steal a loaf most days to take back to his friends. He'd take it from a loaded trolley that would be wheeled around different places. This lasted for a while, after being caught and punished in the Straf he was sent to the steelworks.

At one point in 1942-1943 he worked in a coalmine at 'Hochen Sollen Grooby' which was the most modern mine of the area at that time.

At Stalag 8B he remembered meeting many different characters, for example a football player from Preston North End who would repeatedly bounce the ball from the same place on his head whilst running. Sam met his namesake Sammy Slavin as they awaited punishment. Sammy was from Glasgow, He was shot trying to jump over the perimeter fence probably after drinking hooch. Granny went to see his mother in Glasgow. A friend was Stephen Byers, also of the KOSB from Dumfries. He was 65 in 1942 and had known his dad when he was young.

The fish soup here was memorable, looking like water with heads and fins floating in it. He never had it and preferred to go hungry until the next day. The Germans stopped them singing especially the German National Anthem with 'specially adapted words'. A friend of Sam's tried arguing that it was not the same song but a Scottish one. This did not go down well! After dark the chorus of 'Roamin in the Gloamin' would ring out…Sam remembered it being commonplace to speak backwards to confuse the guards yet communicate effectively.

The beginning and end of the war saw extremes of deprivation. The Long March began in January 1945, before Rabbie Burns night, the 25th, as he remembered discussing the date before leaving. Sam crossed three main rivers and walked the first three days and nights without stopping. In Czechoslovakia he witnessed a fellow prisoner silently asking for bread by pointing to his mouth at locals…and being shot dead for it. On one occasion Sam was lagging behind as his knee was sore and he remembers going over a long, long hill. On the other side was a concentration camp, you couldn't help but walk on the dead, which were 'moving', there were pathetic stick insects everywhere. He met Malcolm (Mad) McGregor there and caught back up with the march.

The March ended at Regensburg in Germany at the Danube. They walked about 10 kms further and found themselves under General Patten. He told them that he couldn't feed them but that they should group in 20s and feed themselves. They took over a fireman's hut and ate his potatoes. Sam came back to Blighty in a Lancaster, over the white hills of Dover, landing at Salisbury. Here he was deloused, given a big meal which he couldn't eat and a rail ticket home, having to sleep on Carlisle station waiting for the connection to Dumfries.

Here he shook hands with Rab Wilson from outside Glasgow, promising to do all sorts with him – only never to see him again."

John S (Jock) Wyllie
Sergeant Major
Regiment's Riding Instructor in the Lanarkshire Yeomanry

Margaret Barbour told me her father's story of life in a Japanese POW camp.

Jock worked for a time as a young lad for John Johnstone at the stables on the Halleaths Estate on the outskirts of Lochmaben. His daughter still has the saddle engraved "JJ " that her father used and the "army reversible bit" belonging to the horse her father rode while in the Lanarkshire Yeomanry. (Bill Hunter, who also lived at Halleaths, remembered his father during the war being told never to plough a certain piece of land on the estate as it had been and would continue to be a race track!)

Jock and his horse, training at Scroggs, Lockerbie in 1938.

Jock had joined the Territorials in 1932 and by 1936 was a riding instructor with the Lanarkshire Yeomanry. In 1940 he was transferred to the 155th Field Regiment – the Royal Artillery. He was self-employed and married to Jean with a baby son before setting off to serve in the Far East.

Jock's daughter, Margaret, told me many stories about her father and the three and a bit years he spent incarcerated in Changi and Taiwan prisons as a POW of the Japanese. She was told by Jim Jackson of Lockerbie that he and his mother had been waiting at the railway station for the returning soldiers and that Mrs Jackson had wept when she spotted the emaciated Jock Wylie. Jock had been a 13 and a half stone boxer, and long distance runner for Scotch Command, and was reduced to 6 and a half stone by the time he returned home.

Jock was visited some 40 years after the war by an old comrade from the camp, Peter Rhodes, a pianist, from Ireland. Peter asked if they minded him playing the piano, despite it needing tuned. He began to play "The Dumfriesshire Foxhounds". This was the tune that Margaret's father had sang which had lifted the men's spirits in the camp. What so impressed Margaret was the fact that the chorus had become such common knowledge to the Gurkhas, Australians and other nationalities in the camp.

"Tally Ho, Hark away
Tally Ho, Hark away
Succession to Dumfriesshire hounds
Hark, hark away."

Another POW musician was Trumpeter Arthur Smith. He would sing, in English, disparaging songs about their captors. One was "Doon the Mine, Bonnie Laddie", a song which recounted the hard labour they had to endure. This included digging a mass grave on the hillside near the camp. The men were told that if the Americans came

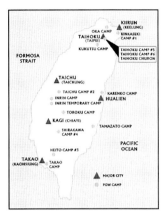

Map of Taiwan showing the POW camps

to rescue them, they would find themselves in that pit. There were even barrels of fuel at the ready. The heads of former prisoners were placed on bamboo fencing and the present prisoners were marched past daily. The last man (usually the weakest) had to replace the service caps that had fallen off the shrunken heads.

Doon the Mine Bonnie Laddie

"British soldiers who had travelled from afar
To fight for King and Country,
Now are prisoners of war.
Tho' your feet are lacerated
And they treat you just like swine'
Doon the mine, bonnie laddie,
Doon the mine you'll go."

Drawing made by a prisoner

Drawing made by a prisoner

Jock was forced to work in copper mines in Taiwan and he saw some of the barbaric punishments which were meted out - men tied to a stake all day facing the burning sun and given a ball of rice laced with salt or being incarcerated in bamboo "sweat boxes" without water. Dysentry and malnutrition as well as tuberculosis all took their toll. Food was a priority for the men especially when the Red Cross parcels did not get through.

Margaret told me that her father used to admire old Jimmy Shanks from Nutholm. As boys he and his brother used to take out a "piece" for him. Once Jimmy accidently dropped the bag of scones into the wheelbarrow which was full of manure for the garden. As boys they were "boakin'" at him eating the piece, but after years in a POW camp Jock reminisced that he had been so starved that he wouldn't have had any qualms about eating a manure covered scone even less the actual manure!

Some of the Gurkhas Jock knew. Many of them signed the back of this card

While in the camp, Jock sometimes crawled through the sewage pipes to get food, cigarettes and hospital supplies from the local Chinese population who were always helpful, but he always gave it to others. His commanding officer, Colonel Jim Fasson, recalled this many times to the family, remarking that Jock could have borne his illnesses better if he'd taken more of the food for himself.

Jock tried to communicate with the guards and used this to try and get easier jobs for the weaker men. He got himself the job of being in charge of the farm because he was keen to try and get food from there for his fellow prisoners. The Japanese had hens which they kept locked away, however with the help of some bamboo poles, Jock managed to sneak away with some eggs. Another time the Japanese had a pig which was being fattened up for their own use. Jock played a trick - not exactly pleasant for the pig, but needs must. He found a little bit of glass and he broke it up and fed it to the pig. Of course soon the pig was in agony and its squeals reached the guards. They asked Jock what was wrong with the animal. Jock examined the pig and pronounced that it had a deadly infectious disease - swine fever. The Japanese would not touch the pig so the prisoners for once had a rare feast.

(Taiwan POW Camps Memorial Society)

Memorial to the POWs of Kinkaseki
(Taiwan POW Camps Memorial Society)

Jock said that the Gurkhas were the "bravest little men". They would be out at night on patrol with them and the British wouldn't see or hear anything, until the flash of blades as the Gurkhas came across the enemy. He also told Margaret that the memory of Lockerbie kept him going. Just before they were captured he and Bill Robertson were in a river swimming for their lives while Japanese bullets were flying around them. Bill had remarked,"I don't think we'll ever see that black woman again". Jock told him to keep swimming! (Bill was referring to the Angel on the Lockerbie War Memorial.)

Jock received a Red Cross parcel from Eaglesfield Girl Guides which contained a knitted square blanket - a god send as it was cold at night. After being freed and on his way home, his few belongings were checked before going on board ship. The American sailor in charge would not let him carry on the blanket as every stitch was covered with lice. Jock, however, never forgot the Girl Guides and always supported their efforts by hosting their summer camps on the farm.

When freed by the Americans, Jock had an incredibly long way to travel home via a hospital in Manila, train across Canada and the Queen Mary to Southampton. He was demobbed in London in 1946 and was given the paltry sum of £75.

He had left Lockerbie in 1940 and only seven letters had reached his wife the whole time he was away. Like many families awaiting news of their loved ones, it must have been hard to keep going and a struggle making ends meet although the Wyllie's neighbours were particularly helpful. (When a soldier was declared missing, his pay was stopped.) During his imprisonment, three times Jock's wife received the letter "Reported Missing, presumed dead", but hadn't known anything about this until she went to the post office to collect her husband's pay. Jock had also missed the early years of his son's childhood, but he managed to carry around and keep safe this photograph (see p45) even though he and his son would not recognise each other in 1946. On that day of his return to Bowmillholm, his son, John was given the day off from St Mungo School and the whole school wrote of his safe return.

Cards from the camps

IMPERIAL JAPANESE ARMY

• I am interned in Taiwan Prisoners' Camp

My health is excellent. ~~usual~~. poor

~~I am ill in hospital.~~

I am working for pay.

~~I am not working.~~

Please see that my life and welfare is taken care.

My love to you

WYLLIE, JOHN.

IMPERIAL NIPPON ARMY

DEAREST. JEAN. AND BABY.
I HAVE HAD NO NEWS FROM HOME. HOPE
EVERY-BODY KEEPS WELL. I AM IN QUITE
GOOD HEALTH, AND NOT DOWN-HEARTED.
KEEP THINGS GOING. JOCK WILL BE A BIG
LAD NOW. HOW IS POP, MARY, ALL THE
REST OF RELATIONS AND FRIENDS TELL THEM
TO WRITE. KEEP SMILING THE SAME AS ME XXX
GIVE MY ALL THE NEWS. LOVE JOCK XXX

Jock and son, John 1940

Jock in 1978

Although safe, he had suffered physically from beri-beri; still had malaria, a bayonet wound in his back and having had the calf of his left leg shot off, he continued to fight to restore himself, yet he never received an army pension. For the rest of his life he was also haunted by many of the horrendously cruel crimes he had witnessed such as the Chinese babies thrown up into the air and caught on Japanese bayonets.

Jock began farming again and continued to uphold the traditions of the Lockerbie Gala as standard bearer in 1961. He attended several reunions of the Lanarkshire Yeomanry in Wishaw. With Jock in the camps were other Scots - some local - Bill Robertson from the St Mungo pub, Chuck Lowther, Mick Lowther (who sadly did not return home), Jim Bell, Bobby Bennett, Kit Carlyle, a chap Gwillim from Dumfries, Joe Wallace, Hector McKie, two men from Sanquhar Willie Williamson and Bill Glencross and Norrie Coupland from Langholm.

Extract

I have just returned from a motoring holiday in Scotland and on my way back to England I called in to see an old Solider whom I had not seen for some years. I say old although he is still only 40.

Perhaps if I tell you his story you may give some publicity to how at least one man who gave his health, is being thanked by a grateful country.

Jock Wylie - 6ft 2ins of brawny Scotsman joined the Gunners in 1930. He was a healthy happy man. He saw action in the North West frontier of India and in 1941 was in Malaya. After various actions there, during which he volunteered for dangerous missions he was captured by the Japanese in Singapore. He was twice wounded, being bayonetted in the back and also shot in the calf. For three years eight months he hung grimly on to life and sanity. Out of 600 prisoners in his compound over 400 died in a month. Burials took place at the rate of twenty a day. Jock Wylie, a kindly character often went without his own meagre, filthy rations to give them to his weaker friends. Once he was tied to a post for hours with his face forced to look up at the sun, escaping blindness by a miracle. ~~He himself was riddled~~ with malaria and dysentry and he still is today.

He came out of the prison camp weighing seven stones, a shadow of his former atheletic thirteen stone. He now stands 5ft 11ins.

He had a wife and a son to come back to and, he thought, a country which would at least see that he would not starve, although permanently broken in health. If you look into the tortured eyes of Jock Wylie you can visualise to some extent what he has been through and also see the disillusionment that lies there.

Jock Wylie has a small holding of just over 40 acres. His son now fifteen has had to do a man's work since he was six years old. Mrs. Wylie broken in health with worry and excessive hard work is bitter. They have a small daughter about nine. Jock has never been able to work properly due to pain in his legs and frequent attacks of malaria and dysentry. In July 1948 after a struggle with the Ministry of Pensions he managed to get a 50% disability pension though he was totally unfit in my opinion. In 1952 this was stopped completely after being whittled away to 11/- per week. He was called to attend frequent medical boards during the period he was receiving the pittance, losing time on the farm which he could not afford. At the boards he was treated like a malingerer trying to get something for nothing. The tortures of his mind did not apparently concern the doctors there.

Jock lost heart and gave up the bitter struggle. Just three weeks ago he went to a Ministry of Health examination and was classed totally unfit for work.

He is one of the finest types of a soldier you could meet. What must a man do to earn his country's gratitude? Jock's natural dignity prevents him going on his knees to beg for a living. A living which this country well and truly owes him.

I am writing to you in the hope that you will publicise this deplorable matter by sending someone like Major Fred Redman to see Jock at his small-holding.

His address is:-

                    J.H. Wylie,
                    Ashyardsgate,
                    Eaglesfield,
                    Lockerbie,
                    Dumfrieshire.

I would be grateful for anything that can be done to see that a grievous wrong is righted.

Testimonial written for Jock by C. W. Dent in 1955

Jim Blackstock
Artillery

I interviewed Jim who still lives in Eaglesfield and learned about his "great escape".

Jim was born at Sandyford, Boreland in 1919. His father was a shepherd who served in the Home Guard during WW2. When Jim left Eskdalemuir School he worked on several farms until he got his driving licence. In 1938 he began working for Johnstones, Livestock in Eaglesfield. When war was declared, Johnstone told Jim he could get him off going into the forces, but Jim was not having that. He signed up and was sent to train at Hadrian's Wall Camp near Carlisle. As he was able to drive he was posted to the City of London Yeomanry which was an artillery regiment - the 61st Light Anti-Aircraft Division.

After training he was sent first to France then sailed to North Africa where he took part in the big push from Tobruk to El Alamein.

Jim and army friends

Jim was fighting beside the Free French. They were being bombed all day and night for a fortnight, but eventually the RAC came in with ammunition. The commander asked for volunteers to take round ammunition for the guns. It was a dangerous job as enemy bombing was heavy. No one was seen to volunteer so Jim stepped forward. For this job he had to move fast so he took another soldier with him to help lift the boxes. As soon as he had delivered the ammunition to one gun and pulled away, a shell would drop behind them. It was as if the Germans were chasing him. Jim received the French Croix de Guerre for his bravery.

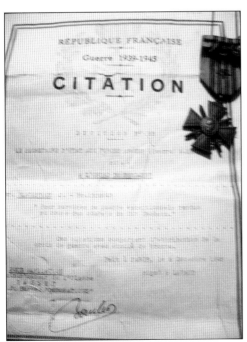
French Croix de Guerre citation and medal

Eventually Jim was captured on 10th June 1942 at Bir Hacheim by the Germans and taken to a POW camp in Italy. From there he was moved on with others to a camp in Germany. They were loaded on to cattle trucks. Two of the prisoners had smuggled pickaxes down their trouser legs determined to hack their way through the wooden floors. They reached the Brenner Pass where German guards came along and shone torches underneath the trucks. They spotted the holes and the prisoners were beaten by German rifle butts. When they reached the POW camp they were scared when they were told to shower because they had heard about the concentration camps, however the guards were trying to get rid of lice.

This was Stalag 1V B which was situated in the Mulhberg area south of Berlin. Conditions were very poor. They only got a ladleful of soup per day and a bun. This diet combined with the hard manual labour in a stone quarry, meant the prisoners rapidly lost weight.

One day two SS officers came to the camp ready to clear it so this must have been towards the end of the war in Europe. The prisoners quickly grabbed what they could and started the enforced march in the freezing cold.

After two days of this Jim and two mates decided that this was enough. They planned to escape by falling behind and rolling into the banking next to a river. The first fellow they met was a German and although he had a pistol, he let them go in exchange for some cigarettes. They travelled by night and soon reached woods where they decided to stay. They made contact with some French workers on a farm who gave them scraps of food and then they built a comfortable hut from wood and straw. One day Jim was washing

POW Jim (Jim is on the left)

in the stream when he saw four German soldiers approaching. Jim decided to brazen it out. It turned out that one of the Germans spoke perfect English. Jim told them he was a British POW and was going to give himself up. The Germans took them into a small town and put them up in a hotel for the night!

They were still in Germany and they needed to catch up with the rest of the British army so they started off on foot travelling north until they spotted some American GIs. They were anxious, having heard that the Yanks were a bit "trigger-happy", so they went forward carrying a stick with a white rag. The Americans took the Germans away, but welcomed Jim and his comrades. One of the Americans came over to Jim and said that the colonel wanted a word then gave him a pack of Lucky Strikes to smoke and his "head spun like a peerie" because he hadn't smoked for so long. The colonel gave Jim a pistol and was told he'd need it to commandeer a car or truck. He did!

They finally reached an army camp and from there they were airlifted in Dakotas to Brussels and from there brought by Canadians to England.

Jim's amazing story reads better than a film script!

Jim's Stalag Dogtag

Jim received several medals including the French Croix de Guerre and he still has his Stalag 1VB dog tag NB Stalag 1VB was huge, but towards the end of the war when the Germans were being attacked both from East and West it grew so big that the POWs suffered consequently from the lack of bedding, clothes and food. The men of Stalag 1VB produced their own motoring magazine named the "Flywheel" filled with drawings and stories. After the war the Russians used the camp to intern German prisoners, but today the camp is a museum open to the public.

After being demobbed in July 1946 Jim returned to work with William Johnstone for a few years. He then went to drive buses for three and a half years, but then went back to Johnstones in Eaglesfield from where he finally retired aged 73!

The Red Cross and St. John's Ambulance sent packages to the POWs including sports equipment and musical instruments.

(from www.caringonthehomefront.co.uk)

(www.wartimememories.co.uk)

"The Long March from StalagXXA in Thorn"   (www.wartimememories.co.uk)

Chapter 3
Women at War

Land girls

During the war there were food shortages due to merchant ships carrying food supplies being torpedoed by enemy submarines and also a shortage of labour on the farms. The Government turned again, as it had done in World War One, to the women of Britain to help the farmers increase their grain and milk production. Many young women signed up for the Land Army immediately. These first recruits went straight to the farms, but later, others were given some initial training.

When the conscription of women began in 1941 many parents didn't want their daughters to join the forces and so encouraged them to join the less regimented W.L.A. (Women's Land Army) or the Timber Corps.

By 1943 there were around 80,000 women working either on the farms or as "Lumber Jills" in the forestry. Their uniform consisted of green jumpers and ties, breeches, brown felt hats and greatcoats. Regulations laid down that each girl was supposed to get a minimum of one week's holiday with pay and over 18s were to be paid a minimum wage of 22 shillings and sixpence.

Betty Harrison in uniform of the WLA.

Some girls in the land army were from cities and unused to country life. One girl had worked as a window dresser in Jenners Department Store in Edinburgh. Imagine the change from that to milking cows! Locally, **Jean Crawford** was in charge of the girls who were billeted at Dinnwoodie Lodge.

John Jardine who lived at Heathfield Farm, near St Anns, remembered his father driving down to collect two girls whenever he needed the extra hands. The two regulars were **Jean Chalmers** and **Betty Sharp**. He said that they all learned quickly and did a good job. However, on **Tom Laurie's** family farm at Carterton they had a land girl who didn't stay too long because, "It was too quiet".

Many of the girls stayed in the area and several married local lads. My aunt, **Elizabeth Shennan** from Lockerbie, became a land girl at Scotsbrig Farm, Middlebie and later married the farmer's son, Kit Blacklock.

I interviewed **Christina Irving, (nee Cairnie)**, who was brought up in Waterbeck. She left school at 13 and went to work on a farm to learn shepherding. When war broke out her father joined the Waterbeck Home

Elizabeth Shennan and Kit Blacklock.

John Cairnie.

Guard and her brother, **John William Cairnie**, volunteered for the navy and served on The Ark Royal and The Illustrious.

Chrissie was very young when she joined the land army and worked on three farms - two at Canonbie and the other at Ecclefechan.

She remembered it being hard work. She had to do all kinds of jobs and at each farm she was the only land girl. On one of the farms there was only Chrissie and the farmer with 35 cows to milk by hand twice a day in addition to the other chores like ploughing and lambing. She did really enjoy it especially looking after the animals like the big Clydesdale horses. There were no tractors so it was all manual work and once she even had the job of tarring the roof of a shed.

She could be working to midnight in the summer with the harvest with no extra pay. (In the beginning she was paid 5 shillings). Chrissie would get one weekend off in a month and she liked to go to the dances at Brydekirk. She'd cycle there, but she still was supposed to be in by 10pm. Once she got back at midnight and she was locked out and had to sleep in the hay shed. A Sunday wasn't really a day of rest as one of the farmers made her join the kirk at Canonbie and she had to go twice every Sunday.

At one farm she had her bed in an attic reached by a ladder. It was like a "bed o' thistles" - the mattress and pillow were full of chaff. "You washed at a sink - no bath, and you had to use the horse trough with cold water to wash your clothes."

Food was the basic farm fare of the time often with boiled barley as a pudding, but if you had rice pudding you had it again - cold in sandwiches in the afternoon. "You were hungry, so it tasted ok." Milk was straight from the cow and there was often an oat drink made from water and two handfuls of oatmeal. Despite the hardships, Chrissie told me that if she had to do it again she would.

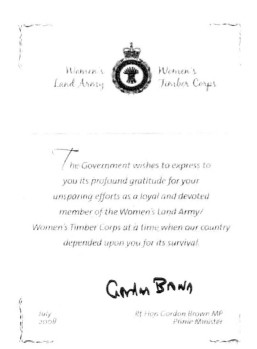

Women's Land Army   Women's Timber Corps

The Government wishes to express to you its profound gratitude for your unsparing efforts as a loyal and devoted member of the Women's Land Army/ Women's Timber Corps at a time when our country depended upon you for its survival.

Gordon Brown

July 2008   Rt Hon Gordon Brown MP
Prime Minister

Certificate in recognition of work done by WLA & WTC.

Chrissie in Uniform.

For many years, Chrissie campaigned for recognition of the work done by the land girls in World War Two. In 2008 she was successful. A medal has been struck for the women who worked both in the land army and the timber corps. In Waterbeck Church the commemorative plaque for those who served in World War Two now includes these local women.

Annie Graham, (nee Shaw), was a land girl for three years. When she left school she looked after sheep and did the milking with her Grandpa at Heugh Hill, so when she became a land girl she was well able to help out at the farm belonging to her

WLA Medal

sister's husband's family the Walkers at Lamonbie. She was the only girl working there, but she didn't have to billet with them as she stayed with her grandpa. She really enjoyed the work and she proudly showed me her recently acquired medal and certificate signed by Gordon Brown.

Girls had to do heavy work and be able to drive. Here is a photo of **Sadie McCormack** at harvest time driving a Fordson Tractor. The farmer is Jock Ewart of Greigsland, Johnstonebridge. These photographs were taken in 1951 as Sadie continued working on the farm after the war. Enjoying a well earned picnic are Sadie, Mrs McKinnel, Bobby Swan and an ex prisoner of war, Friedhelm Gronemeir who was visiting the farm he'd worked on during the war.

Annie Shaw

Sadie McCormack.

Sadie McCormack, Friedholm Gronemeir, Mrs. McKinnel and Bobby Swan.

Betty Campbell (nee Glendinning) now lives in Lockerbie. She wrote down her experiences of being a land girl.

"When I reached 16 I joined the W.L.A. and went to work for Mr Irving at Mouldy Hills, Canonbie. It being a dairy farm, I worked in the dairy, washing all the churns and various other coolers etc, then all were to go in or on a steamer, to kill the germs.

I had lots of duties on the farm, one being feeding the hens and gathering eggs, which were to be washed and graded and stamped, then boxed and sent to the central station to be distributed around the region. The other smelly job was to arm myself with a wheelbarrow, scraper and shovel to clean out the hen houses. Also to put hay in the nest boxes. They were to be shut in at night and be let out in the morning in case a fox gave us a call.

I also fed the pigs with a mixture of vegetable peelings and what was left over from our own meals. Any hens, ducks, rabbits for the table were to be plucked or skinned which was another of my chores, but I refused to do the killing. At lambing time I fed several motherless lambs by bottle, but they were a nuisance, they though they were humans and followed me everywhere.

Betty Glendinning with her friend Betty Harrison and neighbours' children.

There was setting tatties in spring and gathering in October, hoeing turnips and stooking corn (which I hated). Hay time was quite enjoyable, even though we worked till dark on dry nights. I also worked in the farm house to help out, especially at threshing time. It was all hands on deck to feed 18 or thereabouts hungry men.

There were many jobs to do and it was hard work. My day began at 6.30 am, till 7 at night. Once a month I was given a weekend off, Saturday at 11 till Sunday evening. Our only entertainment was the Friday dance, which we looked forward to all week. We cycled many miles and the bands played into the wee sma' hours, sometimes it wasn't worth going to bed, but we were happy and content with our lot.

I look back often to my teens in the W.L.A. with fond memories. We had a decent wage, with working clothes supplied. The only thing I thought was wrong, we didn't get any recognition of our hard work and only now received our badges 60 years later."

It is true that the only entertainment for these girls out in the countryside was the local dance. At least once a week they could dress up and look feminine. "Woman" magazine was popular reading material in the war. It was full of useful cookery recipes and knitting patterns, but also handed out beauty tips. These would be morale boosting for women who found themselves doing men's jobs in men's clothes.

One article in 1942 advised land girls to pack a comfort kit which was to include: "A good embrocation for removing muscular stiffness, and rub it in good and hard (preferably after a hot bath), especially into your shoulders, back and thighs - if you have been digging or hoeing; that's where you'll feel the stiffness most. Put a pound of Epsom Salt in your case too... A pot of vaseline to apply at night to soften hard skin; spirit is excellent for a toughening up process, so put in a little eau-de-Cologne or medicated methylated spirit for rubbing into your palms. You'll find a good antiseptic

Wartime Powder.

plaster is useful for protecting blisters. Put in a pot of rich face cream - a branded one is best (the animal and mineral creams which are quite suitable for your hands might grow hair on your face). Wind and rough weather can be hard on your face and hair too, though you'll find the rain water beneficial. You won't bother with a perm or setting lotion, of course, but you'll cut your hair short and keep it back with ribbon or grip, except, maybe, for special occasions when one or two curlers will help the situation through."

RAF Powder Compact.

Despite shortages there was always face powder. Women carried powder compacts and during wartime some of them were made with the insignia of the RAF or an army regiment. These may have been intended as sweetheart gifts. Essential accessories such as the gas mask (usually carried in a cardboard box) were designed to have some fashion appeal for ladies and stockings were faked using gravy browning to "tan" the legs and pencil to draw a "seam".

Ladies' gas mask bag.

Women knitted and sewed their own clothes. They had to be imaginative often unwinding the wool from old jumpers to knit fresh ones and adapting old curtains to make "new" dresses. They really were following the Government's appeal to "Make do and Mend".

from www.st-andrews.ac.uk/~pv/pv/courses/posters/index/html

Women in the Forces

The war opened up new opportunities for some women to travel or to get the chance to work in a "man's" world. These women did not have to fret so much about their lack of fashionable clothing because they were in uniform. An article in the "Woman" magazine, however, suggested that: "If you are thinking about buying a new hat, try one of the Service Caps". The story then follows three imaginary married women deciding which hat to wear - ie whether to join the WRNs, WAAFs or ATS.

Here follow some wartime stories of women with Annandale connections.

The ATS (The Auxiliary Territorial Service)

Dora Mundell who now lives in Lochmaben is from Wamphray. She was keen to sign up to the army as soon as she turned 18, but wasn't sure which job she would like to do as she felt the only experience she had was helping out at the family post office and shop. She said she was too small to be a driver and didn't want to be a storewoman, but she told me that she chose the right job in the end - she became a cook.

Dora Mundell (3rd from left).

She was thrilled to be sent up to Dalkeith outside Edinburgh for 6 week's training where the girls stayed in wooden huts. She recalled that they all hated dental parade, but if they refused and then had toothache at a later stage, they wouldn't get the treatment.

She was then sent to Leicester army barracks to train as a cook. They were taught by the army instructors using Tommy Aitkens' cook book. These recipes had been used in the famous Lyons Corner House restaurants. Dora was paid 10 shillings and sixpence a week. She gave her mother 3/6d, but Mrs Mundell saved it all up for Dora when she came home.

They started at 4am and catered for over 1000. She enjoyed her work as it was never the same job every day. They had a big room set aside for vegetable preparation; another for butcher meat and a huge bakery with big bakers' ovens. It was all very well organised with a high standard of hygiene. There were some male cooks too.

They had to "Waste not, Want not". Bones were boiled for stock, then the bones crushed for manure. The men and women were rationed bread - 2 slices a day for men and one for women. If it wasn't used it would be collected and dried in order to be made into steam puddings or to coat rissoles. Fat was in short supply and Dora said that they even had to collect it from the sink drains and use it.

Dora remembered seeing the droner planes with gliders attached flying overhead. It was only later when she saw that there were so few soldiers around that it had been a secret mission and all part of the lead up to the D-Day landings. They were always warned about spies and were sworn to secrecy when they took food out to the troop trains – army rations - consisting of sandwiches, a piece of fruit and chocolate for energy.

Dora then moved to Norwich where she was attached to the Royal Electrical and Mechanical Engineers unit and had a "flash" on her shoulders - a bulldog. She cooked in the officers' and sergeants' messes. The canteen there was great and they even had baths. She really liked Norwich where there was plenty going on - lots of theatre visits and dances.

From Norwich Dora then transferred to St Albans to the Royal Army Pay Corps. She remained in the army until 1947 as there was so much administration to be done, but when she did come out of the army she joined the Territorials in Dumfries. She received two medals - one - the King's medal and one - the (young) Queen's medal.

Elsie Wilson

Elsie Wilson (nee Moore) joined the ATS rather than go into Munitions work. She enlisted at Doncaster and was posted to York, Hull and Harrogate. She had been a school kitchen cook before the war and she continued cooking for the men and women at these bases. She had several lucky escapes. Once she was going on a date and asked her friend to do her fire watch, saying that she would return the favour later. She never did get the chance to do that because when Elsie returned the place and been blitzed and her friend gone.

Elsie reached the rank of Lance - Corporal by the time she was demobbed. She had also met **Tommy Wilson** from Lockerbie who was a driver in the Service Corps. Once he was demobbed they married and soon Tommy brought his bride to Lockerbie where she still lives.

Tommy had been a despatch rider during the D-Day invasion. Elsie told me that his brother, Jimmy, was a bit of a dare devil and continued as such in the KOSBs reaching the rank of sergeant, only to lose it then regain it. He was, however, mentioned in despatches for bravery.

Elsie recalled that Tommy had told her about a strange coincidence. She couldn't remember whether it was in France or Belgium or Holland, but Tommy used to give pillion rides to this wee girl who loved the motorbike. He got friendly with her family and was invited into their house. Photos were passed round – one of his brother, Jimmy - and to his surprise the family recognised him - he had been there too!

Tommy had also been chairman of the Lockerbie British Legion and he and Elsie regularly visited the Normandy Beaches on the anniversaries of D-Day.

When **Margaret Nairn (nee McCall)** left school she worked as a clerk in a bank in Dumfries, but she was often bored as the bank was never very busy so when the war began she volunteered for the ATS. I asked her why she had chosen that particular service. One of her friends had enlisted in the ATS as a signaller so Margaret also decided to join and was attached to the Royal Corps of Signals. The girls kept each other company throughout the six months' training on the Isle of Man, but when they reached their posting at Harrogate, they never seemed to come across one another as they were always on different shifts!

Margaret's job was to receive and send messages in Morse Code out in the middle of the Yorkshire moors. She was driven from her billet (in a very nice boarding school in Harrogate) in a lorry for her shifts so that she was well away from potential bombs, though Margaret told me that

Margaret Nairn

when Liverpool was being bombed they could clearly see the sky over the city alight with flames. Her job was really important and some of her messages were the Enigma ones which were forwarded to Bletchley Park to be decoded. She remembered that when the Germans knew they were losing the war they sent their messages in "running hand" ie ordinary German to save time.

Towards the end of the war she was posted much nearer home - to Halleaths and it was whilst there that she met and married a Lochmaben farmer, Robert Nairn.

FANY (First Aid Nursing Yeomanry)

Mrs Ann Bell-Irving, (nee Weatherall), was born in Hampshire in 1925 and brought up in Yorkshire as part of an army family. In 1943 she found herself in front of the recruitment board of FANY. This was the First Aid Nursing Yeomanry to which her mother had belonged in the First World War and was the oldest women's service. (Formed in 1907, it was the first aid link between the field hospitals and the front lines and was given the name because the nurses rode horseback. In WW2 FANY became the Women's Transport Service and a unit for many of the women who served in the Special Operations Executive as spies.)

Athlone Castle   (Wikipedia)

Two questions were asked: "Do you do crosswords?" and "Are you musical?" Ann said she didn't do crosswords and although she didn't play an instrument, enjoyed music. If she'd been a crossword fan then she would have gone into code breaking, but instead she was given the job of wireless operator - in India. At age 17 she boarded the Athlone Castle, a troop ship, to travel to Bombay. It was exciting to be sailing through the Mediterranean and Red Sea.

She disembarked at Bombay and was posted near Delhi via Poona at Meerut. She was "officer status" enabling her to travel first class on the railways and had a room to herself as well as a bearer who would get the water for her tin bath.

Her job was to receive the messages concerning the campaign in the East and send them to the code breakers. As she had learned Morse code when in the girl guides she was quite adept. She worked long shifts - 12 hours at a time.

After a few months, she was moved south to Ceylon where four of them ran their own wireless station in Trincomallee with a small suitcase radio and a charge up battery.

After the war ended she boarded another troop ship bound for home. In 1946 she was demobbed but stayed in uniform working for the FANY Club, in Sloane Street, London, as a secretary. On a trip out to Vienna to visit her brother in 1949, she met John Bell-Irving whose family came from Annandale. After a whirlwind romance they wed.

Ann Bell-Irving

John Bell-Irving

John Bell-Irving had joined up at age 17 when war broke out. He enlisted with a cousin's regiment, the 14th 20th King's Hussars and eventually reached the rank of Captain. He was sent to Persia and Iraq, but felt that he was stuck out in a backwater of the war while El Alamein was being fought. Eventually his regiment was sent to Italy.

After the war he went to Vienna as ADC to the minister, Sir Bertram Jerram. After meeting Ann, he decided he wanted out of the army and take up farming.

John was the son of **Major Bell-Irving** who had served in the First World War. The Major had been in the Imperial Camel Corps and D Squadron of the Lanarkshire Yeomanry. In WW2 he became officer in charge of the Whitehill / Kettleholm Home Guard.

Major Bell-Irving

WAAF (Women's Auxiliary Air Force)

Jessie Richardson

Jessie Richardson (LAC/W) was the oldest of the Richardson children from Lochmaben. Before the war she worked in the laundry at Lochmaben Sanatorium, but sadly that is where she also died.

Young women were being called up and Jessie chose the WAAF travelling down to Coventry to work. Unfortunately she became ill with TB. Her parents went down there to see her in the hospital. One night there was an air raid and they were told to take cover and go to the shelters. Jessie's mum asked about her daughter - where would she go and when she was told by the nurse that patients couldn't be moved, she refused to leave her. They stayed by her bedside all night and in the morning when they looked out the window they saw a great shell hole outside.

Through time Jessie was able to return to Lochmaben, but the TB also returned and she died in 1944. Jessie is remembered on the Lochmaben War Memorial and the family received a beautiful charter from the Royal Burgh noting the gratitude of the people of Lochmaben for her service in the war.

Barbara Grant from Rosebank, Lockerbie was also in the WAAFs. Her sister, Bella, told me that she had a very important job packing parachutes.

Mrs Annie Herrick lived in the Waterbeck area and when war broke out she enlisted in the WAAFs as a driver. She never served abroad, but she was posted the length and breadth of the country and drove lorries, trucks, buses, cars and jeeps for all sorts of army personnel. The work was varied and she recalled that it was a good life, but the best thing about the war was that it was when she met her future husband. He was also a driver for the Air Force, but belonged to Morayshire so Annie believes she would never have met him, but for the war.

Marjory Henderson

Marjory Henderson (Mrs Ross) was born in Lockerbie, but was attending the School of Domestic Science in Edinburgh just before the outbreak of war. She wanted to join Fighter Command and soon found herself off to Kinloss, Oxford and Newcastle for training in codes and ciphers.

After passing her exams she was posted to Acklington near Newcastle. Once they got a call that there was a bandit plane nearby (a bandit was an enemy plane). The plane was going really fast so they would not be able to scramble the planes or shoot the German plane down. The pilot did bail out, however, in Scotland. It was Rudolf Hess!

Marjory's job entailed deciphering the messages that the wireless operators sent through. She had code books but also a forerunner of the computer - a machine called Typex.

She was posted to Cairo in 1941/2 to support the troops in North Africa, travelling in a convoy of 80 ships leaving Liverpool. Marjory was one of 25 to 30 women among thousands of men. The journey took several weeks as the convoy was trying to dodge enemy submarines by sailing almost to Canada and then on to South Africa. There, half of the personnel changed ships. She was fortunate because when the others reached Singapore they were captured by the Japanese.

She found Cairo very hot especially as her work was done underground with no air conditioning. The workplace was called "The Hole". Despite the long shifts Marjory enjoyed her posting which lasted two years. There was a lot of partying and sightseeing and this is where she met and married her husband who was in the army. After the Battle of El Alamein the Germans had almost reached Alexandria and then there was a bit of a "flap". They were all told to get ready their bags so they could leave at a moment's notice and also told to buy something valuable so they could barter should they be caught.

Marjory had reached the rank of Flight Officer and was in charge of a number of personnel in the Levant as well as Jerusalem, Beirut and Haifa where she had a chauffeur driven car to take her round on inspections. One of the saddest messages she ever received was from one of the Dodecanese Islands - " Our last message- the enemy has landed."

The photo of Marjory on p59 was staged and used as a local recruitment poster.

Nursing

Peggy Gibson

Peggy Gibson, from Thorniethwaite Farm, Lochmaben, trained as a nurse in Edinburgh where she became a sister. When war broke out she volunteered for the Queen Alexandra's Imperial Military Nursing Services and was sent to Africa during the war. It was there that she met her future husband - Dr. Hugh Alexander Fleming. After the war they returned to Lochmaben until Dr Fleming secured a practice in Whitehaven. They had a son who became a doctor and a daughter who married a doctor.

War bride

Jean Richardson met Sergeant Alf Baughan of the Canadian Army and they married in 1943. Alf's family had emigrated to Canada from England after World War One. They had a farm out there, but at the beginning of World War Two Alf joined up. Sadly, while he was in the army, his mother died so his army friend, John Rogerson, brought him up to his home in Lochmaben and they stayed with a relative of the Richardsons in Croft Terrace.

They all met up at the dances at Halleaths and when Alf got leave again later, Jean visited him in Brighton where he was stationed and soon after they married.

In 1944 the Government began sending the war brides to their new homes. The Richardson family was not happy as this wasn't exactly safe and Jean would be on her own for a while. Alf, was still on duty in Belgium which meant Jean had to sail alone. Luckily she met a Lockerbie girl, Hettie Kerr, on the same boat. Jean arrived at Pier 21, Halifax and got on a train for Sackville. She must have been anxious about her in - laws, but she needn't have worried. Her father-in-law was there to meet her carrying a big tilly lamp. The Baughan family was really good to her, although life on their farm was tough and the Canadian winters even harder than the Scottish ones.

Jean and Alf returned several times to Britain and on one visit in 1949 they went to Buckingham Palace because Alf was to receive a medal from the king for having captured some Germans.

Munitions Work

Mrs Carruthers (**Isabella McNaught** before she married Ned Carruthers) left school at 14 and came from Palnackie to the Lockerbie area where she worked as a nanny at Briery Hill. She then went to work beside one of her brothers and her father at Jardine Hall home farm where she did the milking. Later she helped set up the building into wards for a hospital for soldiers. She recalled that she didn't really like that and her dad wasn't struck on the idea of Isa joining the land army so she went to work at ICI Drungans in Dumfries. There she worked with the "cotton wool" (gun cotton) making ammunition. After two years she was transferred to ICI munitions at Powfoot where she stayed till the end of the war. This was more dangerous work using nitrate acid. The women had to wear special uniforms: "Blue serge trousers, jumper and boots and metal objects such as buttons, Kirby grips and bra hooks were forbidden." In the photograph, Isa is seated far right in the front row. **Susan Grimrod** from Lochmaben is at the other end of the front row and **Jack Rogers** is standing in the middle at the back.

Powfoot Munitions employed many of the local women. My aunt, **Bunty Shennan**, was one of them and **Bella Grant** from Rosebank worked as a conductress on the buses transporting the women to and from their shifts at Drungans. Alan Hannah's aunt, **Jessie Learmonth**, was employed to repair the clothes of the munition workers.

Powfoot Munitions Workers

Eastriggs Munitions

Another dangerous job for women was the work done at Eastriggs Sub Depot where there was a store of explosives and chemical weapons (Mustard and Phosgene gas). The depot was built up from what remained on the huge WW1 munitions factory.

Women At Home

Women who remained at home did a huge variety of jobs such as nursing; teaching; looking after evacuated children; billeting soldiers (and often their wives and children); organising fund raising events; running social evenings for the soldiers; attending WRI meetings and lectures and serving food in the WRVS canteens, but they also had the difficult task of running their homes on very meagre rations. This will be discussed in the chapter "Home Life".

Typical advert from a woman's magazine in wartime.

Wartime economy recipe
(Annandale Herald and Record)

"Thanks, Mr. Brown, that'll be all right"

After all, when you can't make the particular dish you first had in mind, there are countless ways to make up, and give you meals just as simple, just as nourishing, just as cheap; and perhaps even nicer.

Potatoes, in particular, help provide a variety of appetising and substantial meals and lend themselves to almost every kind of cooking.

Menu Blues fade away

Carrots are another grand standby. Both potatoes and carrots are health-giving, nourishing and endlessly helpful, from breakfast's start to supper's finish — not only with meat and fish but in salads, and even in puddings or as meals in themselves. You can prove it with the tempting treats printed in the next column.

Full recipes for these or other attractive dishes are given in Food Facts Announcements in the newspapers and the Kitchen Front Talks at 8.15 every morning. Or please send a postcard for them to Room 67E, Ministry of Food, London, S.W.I.

BAKEHOUSE MUTTON

Breast of mutton and potato baked together in a simple but unusual way. A very appetising and economical meal.

PIGS IN CLOVER

A novel way with baked potatoes and sausage — a real meal in itself.

CARROT AND POTATO PANCAKE

Just well-seasoned mashed potato with cooked carrot; pan-fried.

CARROT FLAN

Reminds you of apricot flan — but has a deliciousness all its own.

POTATO DROP SCONES

These make a simple sweet for children if served with a spoonful of jam or honey.

Try this one now!

SWEET POTATO PUDDING

Mash 8 oz. cooked potatoes with 1 tablespoon cooking fat, 1 tablespoon honey, and ½ teaspoon salt. Add an egg well beaten and 2 sticks of rhubarb, cut in dice. Bake in a fireproof dish in a moderate oven for about 45 minutes.

Wartime economies   *(Annandale Herald and Record)*

CHAPTER 4
CHILDHOOD MEMORIES

For many children the war was an exciting period. There were lots of new faces in the towns and villages; new friends to make and freedom, for schooling was often for a few hours only each day.

Paul Roxburgh

When war broke out Paul was just a 5 year old schoolboy at Lochmaben Primary and when it had ended he was in what was called the "Control" class taken by Mrs Richardson. He remembers the excitement of there being so many different faces in Lochmaben from the evacuees to the 2000 plus soldiers.

The Home Guard exercised in the field next to the school. One day they had got an old car which they were to attack. They did this with thunderflashes. These devices were lit by striking them against a sleeve which must have had something abrasive attached to it. The resultant thunder and flash caused great drama.

Paul remembers seeing the searchlights from Gretna and then listening to the German planes going over the town at night en route for Clydebank. They had a very distinctive drone - the Heinkels.

The soldiers from Halleaths used to have manoeuvres on the "Beacon" at night time. They used flares which descended on miniature parachutes. Boys would then go over to collect them. (My mother used to make her own underwear from this leftover parachute silk). Soldiers practised house to house fighting in two old houses in Princes Street and Paul watched as men from the Royal Engineers built bailey bridges and pontoons on the lochs. One ranged across the Castle Loch from the Bowling Green to the Yacht Club.

The family billeted 2 Royal Engineers and developed a great relationship - the soldiers had access to sweeties and brought Paul and his brother Rowntrees Fruit Gums.

At Christmas time the boys received presents of hand made wooden "bombers" made by the German Prisoners of War and sold to the locals. Accompanying his uncle in the grocer's van up to Parkgate, he knew little about the Barony Camp - it had a high wall around it so there was some mystery surrounding these prisoners.

Before going out on the round he used to help his uncle sort out the rationed sugar and butter. They knew what their customers would be allowed, for example 2 oz of butter per person, so for a family of five, they made up 10 oz and wrapped it up in greaseproof paper and stuck the name on it. There could be no wastage, but it was a bit more difficult getting the exact amount of cheese rations. You had to cut it very carefully. There were several vans on the road supplying the farms and wee villages and it became tricky when petrol was rationed too. Everyone was allocated coupons for their ration books. The grocer had to take the coupons and send them in to the Ministry of Food. The next month's supply would then be allocated with the number of coupons.

Once when sugar was really scarce, and they were short of coupons, the Roxburghs were asked if they wanted to buy it from the Black Market at 3 shillings a pound. (This was when the price of sugar was normally one shilling.) They were forced to sell the sugar at a loss because only then could they get the supply of extra coupons.

Paul recalls that there were six other grocers in Lochmaben during war time. Eggs were also rationed so the grocers were quite happy to accept eggs and butter from farmers in exchange for payment for their groceries. One hot summer's day he remembered getting eggs and butter from a farmer's wife. She'd put rhubarb leaves over the butter in an attempt to keep the butter cool as there was no refrigeration in the van, but it was fairly swimming by the time the van returned to the shop.

During the war there were two doctors in Lochmaben. They mainly did home visits and Paul recalls one day when Dr Gilchrist came to see him and, to put him at his ease, he'd take the fountain pen out of his pocket and draw a cat on the back of his hand. Here is Paul along with his classmates in 1941.

Lochmaben Primary School 1941

Back row Left to Right:
?,?, Scott Paul, Frankie Wilson, ?, Jimmy Beck, Ian Carter;
Middle row: Olive Lamb, May Green, Addie McGhie, -Little, Nan Hyslop, Margaret Barr (evacuee), ?, Dorothy Ronnie, Joan Burns, Lexa Thomson, ?, Mary Smith
Front row: - Duff, James Grierson, Paul Roxburgh, Roy Thorburn, ?, Robin Richardson, Jim Duff

David Richardson grew up in Lochmaben with his 10 brothers and sisters. He is now in his 70s and living in New Zealand. He remembers being in the secondary department of Lochmaben School during the war years and having a part-time education. He attended school in the mornings while the evacuated children were educated there in the afternoons. Many of these free afternoons were spent around the army bases looking for discarded parachutes or other bits and pieces which might be of interest to boys that age. He certainly feels that he missed out on a lot of his education because of that arrangement.

Bill Hunter of Halleaths Farm
Bill and his brother lived at Halleaths Farm during the war. Living next door to a company of 2000 soldiers was a unique experience. Over 40 acres of the Estate was taken over by the War Ministry and huge swathes of the land was used for training, parades and for the construction of Nissan huts to accommodate the men - and about 60 women of the ATS - from 1940-1946.

The sergeants' mess was just across the road from the home farm so Bill and his brother used to sneak across on summer nights to watch, all agog, the antics of the soldiers at their dances. There is also a deep pool on the estate across which the soldiers had to fix cables to practise crossing arm over arm in full kit. They built bailey bridges which were supposed to stay for a day or so, but Bill's dad persuaded them to keep them for a couple of days longer

Nissan Hut, Halleaths

for his own use. Nearby there still is an ancient oak tree. Some of its branches were cut off by the soldiers to ease the path for their trucks and Bill remembers trying to count the rings and reaching at least 250.

The parade ground was where the present Tile Factory is situated. There are some Nissan huts still in existence and there are concrete bases and pieces of corrugated tin still around the estate - evidence of its former use. Sadly Halleaths House (which had been used by the officers) was demolished and only some of the foundation stones remain.

Prisoners of war were brought from Hallmuir Camp to work on the farm. One Christmas Bill and his brother were delighted to receive two handmade wooden lorries from one of the German POWs. N.B. A former POW, Heinz Roeright became the dairyman at Halleaths Dairy not long after the war had ended.

Bill also remembers one day when they were harvesting oats. The binder worked in a circle with the "island" in the middle getting smaller and smaller and "hoatchin'" with rabbits. As kids they were wise to this, but the watching

Foundations of Halleaths House.

soldiers were patiently waiting for the rabbits to escape and when they did set off running after them. They did catch some!

Ronnie Cunningham-Jardine of Jardine Hall

Ronnie, his sister and his mother continued to live at Jardine Hall during the war, but in the Nursery wing as the rest of the building was used as a convalescent hospital. His mother was matron. She was assisted by several nurses who were housed in Nissan Hut dormitories at nearby Fourmerkland.

Several of the men were Australian - perhaps about 60 men at one time. They were mostly connected to the flying services and sent from aerodromes in England to the comparative safety of Applegarth parish. Ronnie was just a young lad and loved hearing the soldiers' exciting flying stories. The Aussies made boomerangs for Ronnie.

Jardine Hall.

At Jardine Hall Mains - the home farm - there were several land girls and one in particular whom Ronnie adored. Some of the girls worked in the gardens which had to be ploughed up for vegetable growing.

Ronnie's father was away from home. Squadron Leader Cunningham-Jardine who had served in the Flying Corps (later RAF) during World War One had then got the unenviable job of choosing sites for aerodromes thus incurring the wrath of the farmers whose good land had to be turned over to the Air Ministry.

Jack Graham went to Applegarth School during the war. He remembers lots of evacuees, but no evacuated teachers. He also recalled the planes going over heading towards Clydebank and bombs being ditched at Gotterbie Farm on the way back.

Bill Gibson at Thorniethwaite Farm, Lochmaben

Bill recalled finding a grenade on a hill on the farm and playing with it - taking off the cap and picking at the powder - little did he know how dangerous this was. In fact one local boy was killed by a grenade. He also remembers the distinctive "burr" sound of the German planes flying over the farm on their way to Clydebank.

Jean Graham (nee Patterson)

(Jean was the first secretary of Lochmaben P School.)

She was only 9 when war broke out and remembers carrying a gas mask to school. Children were given specially made masks nicknamed after Mickey Mouse, but nevertheless Jean was terrified of them!

Jean's two older brothers both volunteered for the RAF and both survived the war. Bill was a corporal and served in India; Jim served in Bahrain. When they came home on leave it was like Xmas because they had saved up their chocolate rations for Jean and their mother made clootie dumpling, a slice of which they used to take away with them. Jean cried for a day when they left after being on leave.

Child's Gas Mask.   *Photo taken at Dumfries Aviation Museum*

David Knox
David Knox lived in Lockerbie during World War Two. Here are some of his memories of that period:

"Wartime Visitors
In the very early days of the war a number of evacuees came to Lockerbie from Glasgow. Two girls came to stay with us but, when there did not appear any immediate threat to Glasgow, they did not stay long and returned home.

Later soldiers were billeted in private houses in the town and a number stayed with us. The one I remember was Corporal Roy Bellringer, who was, I believe, a boxer of some renown. At the time I remember being very impressed that his wife worked in a HP Sauce factory. (This may have had some bearing on my subsequent career.) Long after he had gone, we heard with great regret that he had been killed in the military campaign in Europe.

At a later stage in the war soldiers came to our house for baths. At one point the Aliens Corps were billeted in Lockerbie and two of their number had regular baths at our house. The one I remember especially was Mr Ronau, who was a German Jew, who had been in a concentration camp in Germany, who had managed to be released and whose wife had then arranged for them to flee Germany for Britain. Mr Ronau had been a prominent Berlin lawyer. He started to teach me German, but alas was posted elsewhere before I had made much progress. Mr and Mrs Ronau settled in London after the war and my mother kept in touch with them for over 30 years."

"German Bombers
I remember lying in my bed one night in, I think, 1941 and hearing German bombers fling above Lockerbie in a northerly direction. I think that they bombed Clydebank that night. Probably because of my innocence at the time, I felt no fear though I did feel a degree of excitement.

In retrospect, I do not think that I had any conception of the consequences of the bombing - the deaths, the destruction, the terror - but then I would only be about eight years of age and of course I had never seen the appalling consequences of bombing locally."

"Victory in Europe
I had gone to bed on the night of Monday 2nd May 1945. Unknown to my family, the press and radio had been told that victory in Europe Day would be the following day, Tuesday 3rd May, and that Winston Churchill, the Prime Minister would make the official announcement that afternoon.

Shortly after eight o' clock, my friend, Ian Wylie (his father was Manager of the Clydesdale Bank in Lockerbie) arrived at our house with a bottle of ginger beer to celebrate the occasion. Needless to say I got out of bed immediately and we duly celebrated the most significant event of my early life with this unlikely beverage.

I had taken a close interest in the progress of the war from 1942 onwards and was delighted that it had ended though I suspect that part of my pleasure was because of the two days holiday from school that we were to enjoy on the 3rd and 4th May. Obviously, there was tremendous public relief and the people of Lockerbie celebrated with dancing in the High Street on the Tuesday and Wednesday nights as they welcomed the end of the conflict and looked forward to the return of their loved ones."

Eileen Gordon lived in Lockerbie in the 1940s. She has written down her wartime memories for her grandson:

"I was 2 years 5 months old when the war started in September 1939, so I don't have any memories relating to the commencement of war.

My parents moved to Lockerbie a month or two before that and my father, who taught English in Lockerbie Academy, was called up to serve in the Air Force in 1941.   He became a Flight Lieutenant, not actually engaged in any fighting, but involved in education in some way, I think.   A lot of male teachers were called up and extra women teachers brought into the schools.   We were living in the house you visited last summer, so were expected to accept incomers as 'paying guests' and one of the incoming teachers (Miss Dunlop) stayed with us, as one of the family, for several years whilst my father was in the Air Force.

Lockerbie - being at a distance from cities or anything likely to be a war target - was home to a lot of evacuees from Glasgow. If you had the room, it was your duty to accept evacuees, and we had two young boys with us for some months. They were brothers, a bit older than I was. Twenty years or so later one of them called in to see my mother and seemed to have happy memories of his time in Lockerbie.

Although we were an unlikely target area, we had to observe the blackout rules: black blinds next to the windows, even in you had curtains inside.   There were no street lights, no lights in the town hall clock, etc. The object of this was that any enemy aircraft would not be able to navigate by identifying towns and villages. [This meant that if you went outside after dark - which was quite early in wintertime - you had to take a torch.] Road signs were removed from all road junctions so that any invaders would find it more difficult to get around. And all window panes - at home, in school, in shops, offices, etc. - had cream-coloured sticky tape top-to-bottom, side-to-side and diagonally across so that if any explosions caused windows to fall out there wouldn't be glass flying around.   You were looking out through little holes in the mesh.   Of course none of that mattered too much to me growing up - it was just normal; but when the lights did come back on that was good. It took years to get road signs back in place.

Lockerbie Infants 1943

Back row left to right:
Elizabeth Brockbank, Andrew Jardine, Jimmy Richardson, Ian Jackson, Robert Shaw, Hugh Anderson, Allan Stoppard, William Nichol, Bobby Gardiner, Raymond McGore, Gwyneth Gass.
Middle row June Scott, Bobby Nicholson, Donald Myatt, Neil Swanston, Eric Nutt, Mary Mason, Bill Muir, Peter Patterson, James Buchanan, Edith Chambers.
Front row Lilias Nelson, Marjory Dyer, June Craig, Susanne Mollison, Olive Cannon, Julia Irving, Elspeth Bollen, Eileen Gordon, Sally Lockhart, Jennifer Wilson, Jeanette Carmichael.

I do remember ration books.   Rationing continued for a few years after the war. I think my mother was quite good at coping with that.   I remember her saying afterwards that she could have paved the streets of London with the packets of dried egg she had used (for baking: scones, pancakes, sponge cakes, etc.).

We had a fairly large garden and we grew potatoes, turnips, beetroot, onions, sprouts, cabbage, cauliflower, peas, lettuce (and I've probably forgotten some).

Children were allowed about 2 oz of 'dolly mixtures' (sweets) a week, and of course we didn't get bananas and other fruit was in short supply unless grown in the UK.

I remember the grocer's boy handing my mother some butter and saying "Put it on and scrape it off!" - in other words, make it go as far as possible.

I remember that food shortages were used by grown-ups to make it hard for children to leave food on their plates, even if they really didn't like it: "Remember there's a war on" - i.e. you're lucky to be getting this food! Sometime after the war finished we had a family gathering in Edinburgh with my grandparents, aunt, uncle, cousins. One of us left a bit of food and my aunt said automatically "Come on, eat up, there's a war on," at which point everyone shouted with laughter - and also with relief.

[My father's brother, Frank, was an army doctor and was sent out to India to look after ill or injured soldiers. At one point his sister's husband (in another branch of the army in India) contracted malaria and was brought into the hospital Frank worked in. I expect this sort of connection happened quite often. It meant that Frank could write to his sister letting her know how her husband was progressing - which was a relief for her.]

I can remember being out in the garden in the dark, with my mother, brother and Miss Dunlop - long after my usual bedtime - the night bonfires were lit on all the hilltops, but I can't recall whether that was victory over Japan (VJ Day) or victory in Europe (VE Day).

I was one of the lucky ones in that my life continued in much the usual way and nothing frightening happened in the locality.

When oranges became available again Ian and I used to be given one to share between us at supper time. Our method of sharing was "You cut, I choose". So if Ian cut the orange I got to choose (the larger bit), and if I cut he got to choose. I reckon that's what made me pretty good at dividing things equally!"

Irene Barbour
Irene Clark (nee Barbour) remembers when she and her friend, Elizabeth Cossar, decided (at the tender age of 11) to make some items to sell in aid of the war effort.

The girls organised a sale of work after persuading Irene's aunt to allow her garden to be the venue. They asked all their friends' mothers to bake or make things for the stalls and run a little cafe too. Irene and Elizabeth made a number of ladies' accessories - felt comb cases and purses as well as necklaces and even felt hats. They earned £27(a good sum in those days) and sent it to Mrs Churchill's Aid to Russia Fund. Irene is very proud of the thank you letter she received from the PM's wife.

Douglas Hannah (Douglas stayed at Lochbank Farm, Lochmaben when he was a young child.) He wrote down his memories of war time:
"My first recollection of the war was the arrival of the evacuees. We followed them from the station to the school where they were allocated to the families who had sufficient accommodation for them... The first refugee rather than evacuee, to arrive in Lochmaben was Bertie Wolff - a German Jew- who stayed (with the Grahams) at Park House. He only stayed for a short time. The large influx of children put a fair strain on the school and for a short spell the local children went to school only in the morning (wonderful) and the evacuees in the afternoon. The church halls of St Margaret's (the Free Kirk) and St Magdalenes (the auld kirk) were pressed into service as classrooms and our schooling returned to normal. Miss Orr was the St Margaret's teacher and Miss Donald from Glasgow at St Magdalenes. All the children got on well together.

At his time the biggest change to our daily lives was the blackout. Looking back to that time our lighting was by paraffin lamp as the gas company had failed just prior to the war and many people did not have electricity. It did not require the "blacking" it would take nowadays. People at that time did not rake about till all hours and young folk were all bedded at a much earlier hour than now.

Fire watchers were recruited and the Local Defence Volunteers was formed. Home Guard HQ was a little house on the west side of Queen St next to George Graham's shop. Conscription for the forces soon took away many of our young men and women and many women were directed to munitions factory at the Broom, Annan. Work started on the aerodrome at Tinwald Downs and the army camp at Halleaths was built. This work was carried out by older men as the young ones were in the forces.

Rationing was introduced and whilst certain things were in short supply those of us who lived in the country did not feel the impact too much. Milk, butter and eggs were usually obtainable and rabbits were in plentiful supply. At that time most folk had a large garden so the slogan "Dig for Victory" did not mean much as so many had been digging for survival since the Depression years.

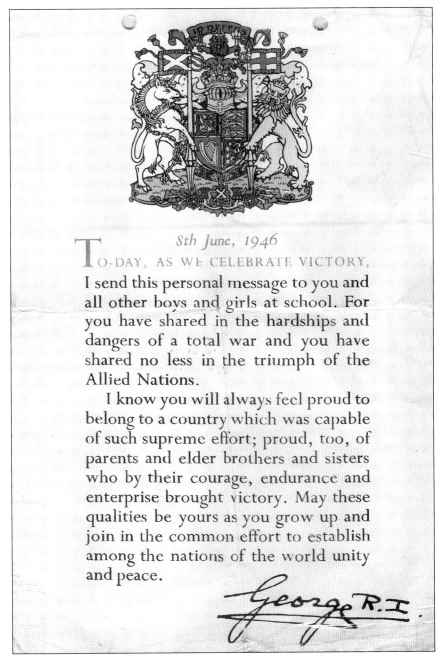

8th June, 1946

TO-DAY, AS WE CELEBRATE VICTORY, I send this personal message to you and all other boys and girls at school. For you have shared in the hardships and dangers of a total war and you have shared no less in the triumph of the Allied Nations.

I know you will always feel proud to belong to a country which was capable of such supreme effort; proud, too, of parents and elder brothers and sisters who by their courage, endurance and enterprise brought victory. May these qualities be yours as you grow up and join in the common effort to establish among the nations of the world unity and peace.

George R.I.

George VI letter to children.

Army training went on all around the area and we were used to convoys of lorries and tanks as well as aircraft circling to land at Tinwald Downs.

As the war progressed we began to receive prisoners of war who spent their days working mostly on farms. At Lochbank there were POWs from Hallmuir Camp. I remember 10 Italians and the civilian driver, Jimmy Wilson hoeing turnips in the old field. I do not remember the hoeing passing so quickly. I remember the prisoners catching frogs when we were cutting rashes in Esbie meadow and this together with an occasional hedgehog lent variety to an otherwise plain diet. It was probably against the rules, but the prisoners all had a meal at Lochbank at lunchtime. The bothy at Esbie was also prepared for occupation and there were 2 German POWs who stayed there and worked full time for a good spell. (Previously all POWs returned to camp under guard at night). Robert and Hans were both butchers in civil life and assisted the pig killing at Lochbank. After the war we received Ukrainian men. One was George Makahon who eventually settled in Yorkshire."

"When the war ended there was a joint church service of thanksgiving held in what is now the Parish Church with the Rev Richard Gibb and Rev Thomas Anderson officiating. It was the largest turnout I had ever seen at the church at that time. I particularly remember it as I rang the bells for the service (the bells were silent during the war) - the Pope's Bell and Bruce's Bell, the oldest bells in the country that are still in use."

CHAPTER 5
LIFE ON THE HOME FRONT

Annandale was no different from other rural areas in Britain in the sense that life at home continued routinely for the most part. People still worked; children went to school; everybody had to be clothed and fed and homes and gardens and farms had to be maintained.

The Government, however, bombarded households with leaflets telling folk to "Make Do and Mend" and "How to Keep Well in Wartime"; newspapers carried Government adverts exhorting the public to do their duty whether it was to enlist in the forces or keep the Home Fires Burning. Information was given in barrowloads about blackouts, rationing, eating well and salvage campaigns. Announcements appeared

This photograph was taken at the Devil's Porridge Exhibition showing a typical home during the 1940s.

about requisitioning of railings and in 1940 the Annandale Herald newspaper carried an article entitled, "Invasion - What to do if the Germans entered the Country". Popular magazines such as "Woman" offered money saving tips to housewives, recipes for making food go further and patterns for turning discarded clothing into the "latest fashions".

Posters such as "Dig for Victory", "Dr Carrot" and "Potato Pete" were displayed in all public places and films, talks and lectures were given on growing foodstuffs. Interestingly research now says that infant mortality went down and the average age of death from natural causes increased during the war and scientists think that the wartime diet with its restrictions on fats and sugars probably contributed to this.

AIR RAID PRECAUTIONS

* The A.R.P. Warden's Post for your Sector is:

C 45

Westmuir 84 at Backcauseway

* The nearest First Aid Post is:

WELFARE WELLS10T ROAD
CLINIC CHAIL STREET

* THESE TWO POSTS WILL ALWAYS BE MANNED DURING AIR RAIDS

Help or advice upon A.R.P. matters will be given by the local wardens.

The nearest SENIOR WARDEN is:

Alexander W Hoggie
A.R.P. NO 1 WARD CE
519 AMULREE STREET
GLASGOW, E.2

Ask him for the name and address of your nearest local Warden and make a note of it here:

Isaac Totten, Snr,
1281, Duke St.

Get to know him *now* and note any changes in the names and addresses given here.

IN CASE OF INJURY
Wounded and gas contaminated casualties who can walk should go direct to the nearest First Aid Post. If you suspect that your clothing has been contaminated by liquid gas, remove the affected garment immediately and place it outside the house, then wash yourself thoroughly. Stretcher cases will be taken to hospitals

GAS MASKS
TAKE CARE OF YOUR GAS MASK. Learn how to put it on and take it off and how to store it properly. Keep it ready for immediate use. If you have no gas mask or if your mask does not fit or seems out of repair, speak to your Warden about it at once.

LIGHTING RESTRICTIONS
All windows, doors, skylights or openings which would show a light, must be screened so that no light can be seen from outside. Do not use a light in a room unless the blind or curtain is drawn, and remember that a light at the back of the house is just as visible from the air as one at the front.

AIR RAID WARNING SIGNALS
● WARNING SIGNAL Warbling or intermittent sound on siren; Whistles blown by police and wardens. ● GAS WARNING Rattles sounded. ● RAIDERS PASSED Continuous sound on siren ● ALL CLEAR. Handbells rung
When you hear the WARNING Signal TAKE COVER AT ONCE and stay there until you hear the continuous sound on the siren

or the ringing of a handbell. Have your Gas Mask with you. If RATTLES have been used warning you of gas, do not come out until you hear HANDBELLS.

FIRE PRECAUTIONS
Be ready to deal with an incendiary bomb. Clear all lumber from your attic NOW, and see that you have easy access to the attic or roof space. Provide two buckets filled with water and, if possible, a stirrup hand pump with two-purpose nozzle, either producing spray for dealing with the bomb itself, or producing a jet for tackling the resulting fire.
Have a reserve supply of water in buckets or tubs. Leave used water in bath.
If you have no stirrup hand pump, have two buckets of sand or dry earth near the top of the house, and a shovel with a long handle for putting sand on the bomb. After covering the bomb with sand place it in a bucket which has a few inches of sand in the bottom, and remove it from the house. Scrape up every particle of burning metal. The resulting fire will then have to be extinguished. Buckets of water or a folded blanket kept wet from a bucket of water might be used.
On no account throw water on the bomb or an explosion may result.

If you cannot put out the fire send for help to

C 45

★ HANG THIS CARD IN A PERMANENT AND PROMINENT POSITION

61-6783

Air Raid Warning.

Wartime knitting pattern

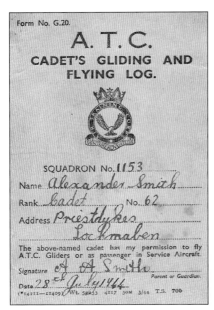

Alec's ATC log

There were dozens of "Bring and Buy" sales and fund raising activities for the Red Cross as well as "Savings Weeks" to encourage the population to buy bonds to pay for military equipment. Local Air Raid Wardens made patrols of houses warning about what to do if a bomb fell and how to comply with the blackout restrictions. Trenches were dug at Annan Academy as an air raid precaution.

Everyone was involved in the war effort:- children were collecting rose hips and helping to gather potatoes; women were knitting balaclavas and socks and McGeorge's Knitwear Factory resumed work in Lochmaben producing navy and khaki coloured gloves for the forces.

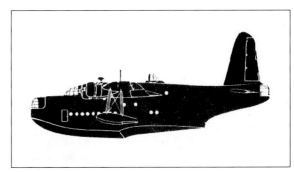

Plane spotter card

Girls also joined up. Here is the Lockerbie Girls' Training Corps in 1943

Youngsters were encouraged to join training corps and learn skills such as aircraft spotting and codes. Alec Smith became a cadet in the Air Training Corps and one night he was taken up to the Gairloch on a training flight. The pilot pointed out the three famous ocean liners, Queen Mary, Queen Elizabeth and the Aquitania all berthed together on the Clyde. That would have been some target for an enemy aircraft!

The Government did introduce several wartime restrictions such as ID cards and the Directed Labour Scheme under which people were often moved out off their jobs to "essential" war work. **Jimmy Graham**, the Lochmaben builder, was rejected by the army because of his dermatitis, but he still made a huge contribution to war work. He was sent to work at the aerodrome at Heathhall near Dumfries and then to ICI making ammunition. This was followed by work at Prestwick Airport and then he was sent to Powfoot and Annan where he worked as a lorry driver. **Alan Hannah's** father worked at Halleaths as a fencer, but was also sent to help build the aerodrome at Heathhall. In 1944 the local papers contained adverts still urging women to join the nursing services.

For some local residents life became very tough. The Government ordained that those

ID Card.

Adult Gas Mask

Model of female ARP warden.
Photo taken at Dumfries Aviation Museum

folk with Italian or German nationality would be interned. This affected some Annandale families like the **Dicerbos** of Moffat.

The father, Tony, and eldest son, Francis were sent to the Isle of Man internment camp where they remained for a year. The locals were amazed as they posed no threat whatsoever to the country.

Tony had arrived in Scotland in 1922 and established a fish and chip business. His son, Emilio, remembered that soldiers used to come down from their cookhouse in the old Buccleugh Garage asking for chips at the back door of the shop. They put them in their hats because of the paper shortages!

On 7th April 1941 disaster struck Gretna. A freemasons' meeting was being held in their Hall – they had come from Annan, Dumfries and as far away as Edinburgh. A bomb hit the Masonic Hall and 38 folk were killed. Another bomb killed a family. Another made a huge crater at the junction of Union Road and Central Avenue. A tale went around at the time that Hitler had targeted the masons in an act of revenge because when he was young he'd been refused membership. What had happened was a lone German bomber had lost an engine and had to offload its bombs before it could land.

Despite all the restrictions and hardships folk continued to attend church, go to whist drives, concerts, dances and the pictures. Cinemas were initially closed for a short time until the Government realised their immense value for showing the news; information and propaganda films and the morale boosting Hollywood productions such as "Mrs Miniver" which told the uplifting story of a family involved in the evacuation of Dunkirk. Even the circus – Robert Brothers Mammoth Zoo-Circus visited both Lockerbie and Moffat during the war.

Neither were the Christmas festivities forgotten. In May 1942 Charley Young (Eggs) Ltd of Powfoot was advertising for people, "To rear Geese, Turkeys, Ducks etc. for the Christmas demand."

Several of the large houses and estates in the area were commissioned for war service. The Royal Engineers and the Commandos had their HQ at **the Dixons**, Lockerbie. The soldiers from there regularly attended the picture house - the Rex - in Lockerbie or

Cinema Advert from local newspaper

"smokers" - evening entertainments at the Rex Restaurant in Lockerbie. Dances were held as well as sports and there were always sandwiches available at the canteen opposite Dryfesdale Church.

Violet Nelson lived at the Dixons and she remembers that one day the Commandos were there and the next morning they were gone. No one knew where. She also remembers the old Colonel – Bickey - who used to smoke his pipe after dinner in the field where the bull was. Most of the men wouldn't have dared go in there, but the bull never moved when the colonel was there. He was also an extremely quiet man.

One day the colonel instructed his driver to take him into Dumfries to Lennox's, the wine merchants, in the town centre. The driver waited for him while he went into the shop. The driver thought he heard him come back into the back of the car and so drove off. When the car arrived at the Dixons, the driver discovered that there was no one in the car - he'd left the colonel behind in Dumfries!

Halleaths, Lochmaben

Halleaths Army Camp was built and then finally demolished by the Royal Engineers who were first billeted in the Church Hall in Lochmaben before using the camp

Halleaths House

themselves. During the war it was used almost continuously. Halleaths House which had been built in 1843 by Dr Andrew Johnstone was used as an officers' mess. There were huts everywhere: - a NAAFI canteen, a parade ground, minefield, shooting gallery and two rifle and machine gun ranges. **Alec Smith** remembered working in a field nearby when his pal told him to duck down and cover his head with his jacket. Soldiers had appeared wearing gas masks and gas was being released on the assault course next to them. (Presumably it was something safe like laughing gas.)

Alec recalled that the family were friendly with the soldiers and some would even help out at Priestdykes (the

Harry Briddon

farm is next to the camp) at threshing time. One day one of them asked Alec if he'd like a haircut – it would cost him a few cigarettes. As Alec didn't smoke he got his mum to buy them. Once he'd acquired the goods, he rushed out with a towel around his neck. The haircut was fine, but the soldier then proceeded to give him a shave with a cut throat razor. This would be Alec's first and last time although he admitted it was a perfect shave.

Another story he told me was about the time the train dropped off a quantity of railway sleepers for mending a fence. Next day the labourers came to fix the fence to find only the nails and the metal wheel of the barrow. It must have been cold because the soldiers had had a grand fire that night.

The photograph here shows a young soldier at Halleaths Camp. He was Private **Harry Briddon** of the Lancashire Fusiliers from Blackpool. Harry was billeted with a family in Queen Street, Lochmaben and coincidently was the uncle of Dr John Wilson who now lives in the burgh.

The Reconnaissance Corps was formed there in January 1941 and it was here too that the SAS was formed which was eventually named 2 Commando. It was a large recruitment centre and there used to be a sentry box at the Lockerbie Road entrance near today's bus shelter. There is more information about Halleaths in the chapter "Children's Memories". **Madge Jardine** remembers a maid at Lochpark being friendly with a soldier at Halleaths. She'd been complaining of the cold and returned from her date with 2 blankets - a navy blue and a khaki one - never to be returned to the army.

Wilma Twidale remembers huge numbers of soldiers coming into Lochmaben and a canteen being set up for them using both the Church Hall and the Town Hall. Lochmaben Town Council minuted a plea in 1940 for the burgh to billet Norwegian soldiers. The town was, however, pretty well full and so the Norwegians' request was denied and they had to look further west for their accommodation. The council, however, recommended that, "Condemned houses would be granted to tenants of bombed areas and soldiers' wives."

Lochmaben Golf Club was also taken over during the war for exercises and training of the Royal Engineers. No golf was played there for five years. The engineers from Halleaths erected the wooden structure for landing boats at the Kirk Loch, which along with the Mill Loch were regularly used for training. According to **Jim Twidale** there is still a PU Van in the depths of the Kirk Loch.

Chapelcross Farm outside Annan was converted into an air base for wartime use, however it never returned to farmland, as it became the site of a Nuclear Power Station that only recently was demolished.

Jackie Paterson, the British World Champion Flyweight Boxer, was stationed at Chapelcross when he joined the RAF.

Sadly a number of British aircraft crashed in the region, often when on training missions. There is a comprehensive list in the Ewart Library, which includes two "Hurricanes" which came down near Cummertrees and two "Battles" near Johnstonebridge.

Hoddam Castle.

Hoddam Castle was used for Tank training and **Milkbank** was home to the Argyll and Sutherland Highlanders and the Black Watch. Some of the larger estate houses were commandeered by the MOD to be used as hospitals such as **Rosebank** on the Castlemilk Estate and **Dormont House** in Dalton; **Dryfeholm**, **Jardine Hall** and **Wyseby House,** at Kirtlebridge, were used for convalescing officers.

Hannah Moffat said that her sister-in-law used to work in the NAAFI at **Kirkconnel Hall** which had become a rest home for performers and musicians before they went off to the Fronts to entertain the troops.

Rammerscales at Hightae, **Raehills** near Beattock and **Comlongon Castle** were all temporary homes for evacuated school children. Australians were stationed at **Dryfeholm** and taken every day by truck to cut timber. They weren't even supposed to be here. They originally were to go to the Middle East but were brought to Scotland instead. Many were bushmen and stayed about 2 years,

Rammerscales

The Battle School

but some remained and married local girls. Other visitors who came over to help the war effort by working, as lumberjacks were about 200 men from British Honduras. They lived at the lumber camp at **Kirkpatrick Fleming**.

6 Troop

Moffat played host to a number of soldiers from different regiments who had been selected because of their specialist skills to join The Battle School. The soldiers were lodged with families in the town. Two of the men from 6 Troop stayed with **William and Annie Duncan**. Their son, Billy, remembered that they never used either the front or the back door, but scaled the rone pipes. This would have been part of their training in the Special Services (SS). Another was to aim their "long daggers" at a scarecrow image of Hitler in the Duncan's back garden.

Moffat had been chosen because of the similarity in terrain to that of France. These soldiers had been sworn to secrecy and couldn't let their hosts know where they were off to. The evening before they left they told Billy's parents that they might be away a couple of days. Sadly they were never to return. All but 2 men of the 6 Troop fell at Arnhem in the Netherlands.

Moffat House

Moffat House was used as an officers' billet where there was an assault course in the garden and the boating pond at Station Park was also used for amphibious training.

Bob and his family

Emilio Dicerbo told me the story of the guard at Beattock Station who had been ordered to black out or cover up all signs (all stations had to do the same) as there would be a train coming through with German prisoners en route north and the army didn't want the prisoners to know where they were.

The train came to a halt at Beattock to get water etc for the climb up the summit when loudly came the usual call from the guard, "Beattock Station, all change for Moffat!"

Annandale folk opened their homes to many different groups of people who came to the area. In other chapters the stories are told of the evacuated children; the land girls and the POWs who lived and worked in the towns, villages and farms of Annandale, but there were also the wives and children of soldiers who were billeted in the area. Many were grateful for a chance to be near their loved ones before being sent abroad. Often they returned to Annandale after the war to visit their former hosts. My maternal grandmother, **Flora Shennan**, was widowed during the war, but loved having these visitors whom she squeezed into her council house in Lockerbie. The photos shown overleaf are soldier, Bob, and his young family shortly after the war.

The postcard shown below was sent by a soldier possibly to his sister reassuring her that he was safe and well and in Lockerbie. Let's hope he survived the war to tell her more about Annandale.

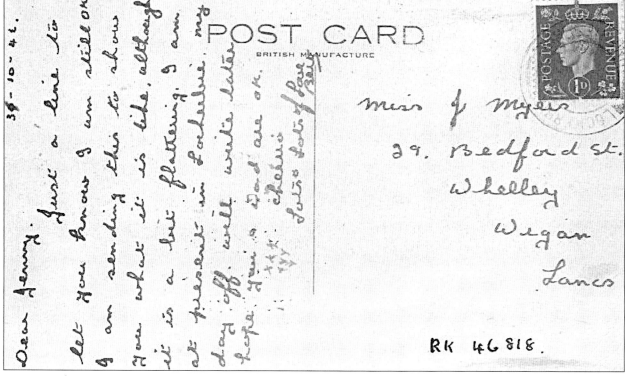

"But I've GOT a radio set!"

MURPHY 70 TABLE MODEL All-wave superhet. Each waveband on the scale is illuminated in a different colour for easy tuning. Alternative aerial sockets to suit local conditions. Variable tone control. High standard of reproduction. Really good value for money.

Yes, Sir, but they say it may be a long war—may last for 3 years or more. Will your present set work perfectly for as long as that without letting you down when you need it most? If you have the slightest doubts on that score, *now* is the time to get a new set, and for goodness' sake make it a Murphy. We think it's the most reliable set you can get. We hold good stocks now, but we don't know how long they'll last because the demand is pretty high everywhere. Anyhow, it's better to be on the safe side and get a pre-war Murphy *now*.

Cash Prices:
STANDARD MODEL £10.5
PRESS-BUTTON MODEL . . . £12.0
(DC/AC models of above 5/- extra)
ARMCHAIR CONTROL MODEL . £13.15

You have a choice of 40 sets in the Murphy range, giving Manual, Press-Button and Armchair Control tuning.

YOUR **MURPHY** RADIO DEALER

All Murphy sets, exclusive of valves and batteries, are guaranteed for one year.

THOMAS DUFF
Ironmonger and Electrician
LOCKERBIE Telephone: 24. **ANNAN** Telephone: 18

The Government was keen for everyone to hear its information broadcasts and encouraged the use of radios

(Annandale Herald and Record)

Chapter 6
Evacuees

Evacuation

Fear of the Germans bombing Scottish cities and docks spurred the Government to plan for the evacuation of children from Edinburgh, Glasgow, Rosyth, Dundee and Clydebank. They were advised to take a gas mask, change of underclothes; night clothes; house shoes or rubber shoes; stockings or socks; tooth brush and towel; soap, face cloth; handkerchief, warm coat or mackintosh, tin cup and a parcel of food for a day. For them the war started on the first of September. This was Operation Pied Piper.

On the day of the first evacuation 419 children from the Dennistoun area of Glasgow arrived in Lockerbie. They were met by the Town Clerk and served refreshments in the Town Hall by various Women's Guild members. Most of the children had attended Wellshot Academy in Shettleston.

At Lochmaben there were 399 evacuees - 240 for the burgh and 159 for the landward area. They came from Newlands School in Parkhead. Several children were evacuated to Hightae where they were able to sample the luxury of Rammerscales House.

The local newspaper ran a story a week later about the reactions of the city youngsters to country life. "Two... youngsters from Glasgow who are enjoying their stay in Annandale are Robert and Fred"... "At first neither could understand why it was that hens didn't lay twice a day. Fred came in triumphantly the other morning with a basket full of what he called "unbreakable eggs". He had gone round all the nests and gathered the pot eggs!"

Some children came by private arrangement often to the homes of rural relatives. **Mrs Isobel Maxwell** came to the Boreland area. She hated it and returned to Glasgow after a very short while, however, by then she had met her future husband and eventually returned to the area to be married. She still lives in Annandale!

Evacuation was planned in great detail from the timing of the trains, the organisation of the reception committees and the exact numbers of children each parish was to take. Payments were made to those who billeted the children and some provisions were made for accompanying teachers who were advised to: "obtain the use of a bicycle" as there would be no petrol allowance.

One famous teacher who came with his class from Strathclyde Primary School to Moffat was the author **Robin Jenkins**. In his novel "Guests of War", the town of Langrigg stands for Moffat.

Organising the intake of evacuated children was one of the first tasks for the newly appointed headteacher, William Coulson, at Johnstonebridge School. Several children came and went away again in the first few months of the war, including two private evacuees from Glamorgan, Wales, but in April 1941 twenty children arrived from Glasgow and in August more children arrived with their teacher, Mrs Andrews from Goodhope School. Space had to be found for them in Johnstone Church Hall as the school was cramped enough with the 63 local children.

A young **Jock Graham** remembered feeling sorry for "the puir wee souls" who arrived at Applegarth School not knowing where they were. Not quite an evacuee as such, was **Jim Neill**. Jim's house in Clydebank was blitzed and left the family homeless. His father was a soldier and was posted to Halleaths so Jim and his mother came down to Lochmaben to stay in a room in old Dr. Gilchrist's house on the High Street before finding accommodation on Princes Street. One of Jim's earliest memories is of a tank thundering up the High Street. Jim was only four when he left Lochmaben, but has now come back for good.

Sadie Cockburn was waiting for a postgraduate teaching course to begin at Jordanhill College in Glasgow when war broke out. She believed that she had a month to spare before college so she applied to the call for voluntary helpers. She was accepted and told to report to the nearest school, St John Neilson Cuthbertson School, to prepare for evacuation en masse. No one knew where they were going when they took the train at Pollokshaws East Station. The ended up in Lochmaben and she and four children were taken by **William Hunter** in the car to the farm at Halleaths. This was the beginning of an everlasting friendship.

Sadie was to accompany the children to school a mile away and make herself useful. When October came Sadie contacted the college and was able to secure her teaching practice at Lochmaben. She was thrown in the deep end as she was "attached" to the Headmaster's class, but as he was also the provost, Sadie was often left to get on with the teaching herself. Much to her delight, Sadie was able to complete her training in Lochmaben as Mrs Hunter was expecting a child and already Sadie was feeling part of the family. Sadie did leave for another post, but not before becoming Bill Hunter's godmother. At age 92, Sadie still makes the train journey down from Ayrshire to visit Bill.

Raymond Kirkbride and his two sisters came to Lochmaben with their Mum in 1939/40. They had connections with the area, as Ray's mother, Jane Blyth, was the daughter of a local man, John Cowan. They first lodged with the Storey family in Halliday Terrace, however they needed a larger house so they got the use of downstairs at no 30 Princes Street. This house had been condemned and the upstairs was boarded off, but they still had 2 rooms and a kitchen. They had an outside toilet and paraffin lamps for lighting.

Raymond's father was in the navy and when on leave in 1942 he was walking down Princes Street when he met the minister, Mr Gibb. The Reverend Gibb asked him, "Can I give you a lift?" perhaps thinking that he was far from the sea, but Ray's dad replied," Only to number 30!"

Raymond and his sisters.

Unusually for an evacuee, Raymond attended Lochmaben Primary fulltime and didn't go to the annexe. He'd come from Kennedy Street School in Glasgow's Townhead. He found out later that his Glasgow school had marked him down as absent instead of being present at Lochmaben. He remembered receiving a prize book for General Excellence. It was "Black Beauty". He recalled some of his teachers - Miss Murray, Miss Carmichael and Mrs Mitchell.

Raymond had fond memories of Lochmaben folk. He felt accepted and at home there. The evacuees were well integrated and he became good friends with John and Scott Paul. For entertainment Raymond liked the cinema. He would board the bus at 1.30 every Saturday to travel to Lockerbie to the Rex Cinema. He'd return on the 5pm bus and go into McMichael's in Queen Street to get the broken biscuits. Later in the war he would only have to walk up to the Barras Cinema to see a film.

He earned some pennies by helping John Paisley deliver papers round the town as well as run messages for two old ladies after school. Raymond remembers many of the shops in Lochmaben that have now disappeared for example Duff's, which became Jepson's, on the High Street. Raymond loved his comics especially the "Beano" and "Dandy". Children didn't think about the war - they had their bikes, but they also had their illicit cigarettes. Raymond remembered "an old worthy" who lived in an ancient cottage and had an "open door" for cigarette smoking!

Jean McCauley (nee Malcolm)
Jean stayed with the Graham family (the builders) in Lochmaben until November 1940. This was the year of the "phoney war", but like many children the family were evacuated again in 1941 once the Germans started bombing raids over the Clyde. This time it was to Lanarkshire, but although there for 2 years she felt she did not make the lasting friendships she had done at Lochmaben.

The photograph Jean sent is of the families waiting in the schoolyard to be evacuated. Here she tells her story:

Glasgow Evacuees awaiting their train.

"September 3rd 1939 will always stay in my memory. That morning there was a lightening storm and a barrage balloon caught fire and tore away across the sky. All the children assembled at our local school with their little suitcases and gas masks and then we were issued carrier bags with 48-hour rations. All I remember of the contents are Kit-Kats, Marie biscuits and corn beef. To this day I associate Kit-Kats with the war. My mother and aunt were accompanying us - we were three - my cousin Netta Kay aged 13, my brother, Bill, aged 5, and me aged 9. We were hoping to be billeted all together. We all walked in procession down to the local station, the road lined with people, mainly women, all in tears. We changed trains at Lockerbie for Lochmaben though I doubt anyone knew exactly where we were. At Lochmaben, T.D. Brown, the Town Clerk was on the platform organising things and we eventually got to the school. My mother afterwards referred to the proceedings as "the cattle auction"!

Andrew Graham decided on us right away but then he discovered that there were three of us. Nothing daunted, he scooped us all up and took us to the Moorings - I'll never forget Bella Graham's expression when she saw us. She said, "Andrew, what have you done? I said I'd take just two." She rallied quickly, however and made us all welcome- a warm-hearted woman. I remember Netta and I were so impressed. There was a big log fire. We'd never seen a log fire before except in the movies. Glasgow had coal fires. Then there were the large oil lamps and later the candles to light us up to bed. This was like a fairy story to us. We were fascinated.

The garden too delighted us and the hen run and the orchard, all so new to city kids brought up in flats. There was a dog, Miffy, who was half blind and a cat. My mother and aunt returned to Glasgow, but my mother returned - perhaps after Christmas as a B helper and stayed for some months. Lipton, the tea man, ran buses on Sundays for parents to visit their children, probably once a month.

We started school right away, Bill and I at Lochmaben and Netta at Lockerbie. I can't remember now how long Netta stayed in Lochmaben before returning to Glasgow. Bill and I made friends very quickly and settled happily into country living. My close friend was Jean Graham of Gowanlea and we spent a lot of time together either roaming around the Castle and Mill Lochs or out at Gowanlea sailing boats in the burn. I was constant visitor out there. This friendship survived the war.

In the evenings I read Burns' poems to Uncle Andrew. I also ate delicious potato scones. I got to feed the hens too. Bill and I played in the sand pit and a swing was put up in the woodshed for us. The workmen used to eat lunch there and they would whittle little utensils for us. If I couldn't be found outside, everyone knew where to look for me. There was a back room, which probably had been a maid's room, and it was my Aladdin's Cave. There was a sideboard full of books and I managed to read quite a lot of them. It was said that my ghost would walk with a book in my hand.

That first winter was very severe. There were huge snowdrifts and then the Mill Loch froze over. On one of my father's weekend visits, I watched him curling on the loch. Driving to Dumfries (to Binn's, where else?), the snowbanks were higher than the car. Of course all we children loved the snow. The winter finally gave way to spring and I found my first snowdrop under a hedge - odd the things one remembers. I remember too the milk being delivered by pony cart - very exotic! Sandy Cowan, Andrew Graham's nephew brought it every morning. Does anyone remember the glove factory house in a little building on Princes Street I think - past Crolla's cafe? Sometimes Mary and I would walk round the "wee O" in the evening. In the holidays, Andrew Graham would take Bill and I with him out to farms where work was in progress. We got to collect eggs.

Glasgow neighbours of ours had three teenagers billeted in Balcastle so we played a lot there too. Mrs. Brown gave a Hallowe'en party for the evacuees of the High Street. The saddest evacuees were Bertie Wolff and his sister. Their mother had got them out of Germany but they didn't know whether their father was alive or not.

A little amusing memory - one summer evening Bill was late for supper. He said he and his friends had been playing at the old castle in the back lane when they saw fairies dancing in a ring. Lochmaben magic?

The school term ended and I came first in my class. Andrew Graham found out that they weren't going to give me the prize because I was an evacuee. He was furious and confronted the committee - I got the prize.

My sister was born in August 1940 and we had a seaside holiday to see her. I guess that made us homesick so we left Lochmaben in November 1940 - the war was pretty quiet at that time. It seems amazing that we were only 14 months in Lochmaben - it seems as if it were longer, it was such a new experience. We couldn't have been billeted with a better family and we were treated as members of that family - a kind of younger brother and sister to Mary and Jimmy. It had quite an impact on our lives. In my teens, I spent summer holidays there, rode a donkey down the High Street when they had a Fair to raise money for the homecoming soldiers in 1945. Later,

I went to dances in the country with Jean Graham and other friends, swam and rowed on the Castle Loch and even climbed Beacon Hill."

The photograph is of Lochmaben School with a teacher called Miss Margaret Murray who came from the Western Isles. Included in the photograph are Jean Graham, Joyce Richardson, Simon Smail and Ken Wright as well as Jean.

Lochmaben Primary School with the evacuated teacher.

Alan Hannah

Alan remembers some of the evacuees who lived in Lochmaben. Some came privately. He remembers some names which will likely ring bells with Lochmaben folk- William Skirving who stayed with Mrs Baxter in Queen Street; Adam Millar who stayed with Mrs Blackstock and could turn somersaults down the street; Colquhoun with Mrs Harkness; Howat at Croft House and Robert Moodie at Balcastle with TD Brown who was the town clerk.

Robert Moodie wrote an article, which was published in the "Dumfries and Galloway Standard" on September 22nd 1999 marking the 60th anniversary of his evacuation. Robert remained in Lochmaben for six years and had fond memories of the burgh. Lochmaben folk remember Robert who went to school with them, skated on the lochs with them and sang solo in the church. In the article Robert mentions witnessing the crash of a Hurricane fighter plane over Hightae.

Jean Bower

Jean Bower, **nee Langley**, was born in Glasgow. She was first evacuated at the start of the war with her two brothers, but returned to Glasgow during the phoney war. Jean tells the story here in wonderful detail of her second evacuation to Corrie near Lockerbie.

"1941 – this time my oldest brother stayed at home. It was the same procedure as the first evacuation, no idea where we were going. Off we went with our labels, gas masks, etc."

We ended up in a very small village called Corrie, six miles outside the market town of Lockerbie and lined up like cattle in a church hall waiting to be picked. My first billet was on a farm where after a short time the family decided they only wanted one child, so my brother stayed and I was sent to stay with the schoolmistress and her housekeeper.

This was a very strange and lonely experience for me. A mistress/servant experience, which I never been exposed to before. The schoolmistress was served and ate in the front parlour and the housekeeper and I ate in the kitchen. There was little or no communication. As I look back it is strange to think of the Upstairs/Downstairs syndrome with only two people in the house. There were no children to play with, it was very lonely. When school vacation time came the schoolmistress had to find me another home as she was going to visit family in another part of Scotland.

I was delighted when I was taken to a small, white, two - bedroom cottage, at Corrie Brig, two miles from the little village of Corrie, but this time with a family who had five children, all older and working except one daughter who was a year or so younger than me. I had a playmate at last.

The McCaughie family was a very happy, kind and friendly family, but, another culture shock… Mr McCaughie was a gamekeeper for Sir John Buchanan Jardine and wore a uniform … if you could call it that…lovely check tweed suit with plus fours, collar and tie and heavy brogue shoes. He always looked very smart. I was too young to have heard of the book, "Lady Chatterley's Lover"!

The family lived rent free, but must have had a small income. Their son worked on a local farm and three older daughters worked at Jardine Hall, a lovely, large mansion that had been converted to a convalescent hospital for the services. On their day off, the girls cycled 15 miles each way to visit home.

What does a gamekeeper do? From what I remember Mr McCaughie, caught game, rabbits, grouse, pheasant for the Big House and looked out for poachers, which was ironic as the son used to go rabbit catching with a ferret and traps and Mrs McCaughie made lovely rabbit stew. I've never understood people having ferrets for pets. These ferrets were trained for hunting and were nasty little things.

Mr McCaughie had two hunting dogs, lovely black Labradors that we were not allowed to pet or play with. However there was old Ned a lovable Cocker Spaniel. Ned was supposed to a hunting dog, but of course was not in condition and really the house pet. One day Mr McC decided to take Ned on a days work. Off they went, Mr McC had his game bag and his rifle over his shoulder and old Ned by his side. In the late afternoon, we were not to laugh as we saw Mr McCaughie coming across the field carrying an exhausted old Ned.

Corrie Brig was a two - bedroom white cottage, with an outside toilet, no electricity… in a lovely peaceful valley surrounded by hill farms. I didn't seem to mind the lack of these modern conveniences. There was very little socialising, but everyone helped each other at harvest and hay time, sheep shearing and dipping, and all other farms events that needed help. I remember one very severe winter when the roads were blocked watching a convoy of farmers with their Clydesdale horses and carts walking into Lockerbie to get provisions.

The McCaughies had a radio, powered on a wet battery, which was exchanged weekly by the grocer. We listened religiously to the news and Prime Minister, Winston Churchill. The family loved music, Scottish and Irish and I remember listening to Irish tenors of the time and learning the songs.

The son was a wonderful accordion player and had never had a lesson. On a good summer evenings he would play outside and music drifted down the valley and up to the farms on the hills. A lovely memory.

The family was always busy: Monday was wash day. The big boiler in the kitchen was lit early and the clothes hung out on the line. It was almost a competition in the area as to who had their clothes out first. Tuesday of course was ironing, two days were baking days, different household chores on the remaining days, of which we had to help when not at school. Everyone worked hard and house, clothes, etc. were spotless, hand sewn and mended. When not at school, we wore clogs, leather uppers and thick wooden soles that had metal attachments (like a horse shoe) on the soles and heels. I don't remember them being uncomfortable.

How the women managed their delicious baking on a paraffin/kerosene stove and cooking over a fire, I don't know. The butcher and grocer vans came twice a week; the draper came about once a month, but much of their food was home grown or made. They had a cow and made butter, a pig which a local farmer had provided for them and helped them slaughter and cure, hens and bantams, a lovely vegetable garden and of course,   Mr McC and son Jim provided wild life. We had pheasant at Christmas. I didn't realise until many years later what a delicacy it was.

During the summer we had to spend our Saturdays and Sundays picking fruit in season, which grew along the hedgerows at the side of the road: gooseberries, blackberries, wild strawberries, raspberries and black and red currants. Mrs Mc C made the most delicious jams.

Corrie saw little of the war, though we did have tanks and army lorries (vans/trucks) drive past on manoeuvres. There was a Home Guard which met once a week, land girls who worked on the farms and Italian/German prisoners of war who also worked on the farms. After the war, Jim McCaughie, the son married Elsie a land girl from Glasgow.

Towards the end of the war, there was a day of great excitement, Sir John Buchanan Jardine and his entourage arrived on horse back for a fox hunt, which Mr McC had arranged. They stopped very briefly at the cottage to thank the family who all felt very honoured.

When it was time for me to go High School, I went to Lockerbie Academy of which I only have happy memories. The little town was over-crowed with soldiers from camps all around. Lockerbie is a lovely little clean market town with a few very old hotels. Thursday was Market Day and on our lunch hour we would go to Market Place to see the animals that were up for sale. Lockerbie hasn't changed too much. I love to visit when I go home to Scotland and still keep in touch with the remaining members of the McCaughie family.

I stayed with the McCaughie family for three plus years and returned to Glasgow with a very strong Dumfriesshire accent and dialect which I had to lose quickly when I returned to high school in Glasgow.

I read this to my six year old granddaughter – the only one I could get to listen to me and she asked me a very insightful question for a six year old: "Didn't you see your parents in all this time?" I explained that my father arranged coach trips with other parents to visit Corrie and also I had to write home every week and my mother sent me pocket money, every week for stamps and essentials. I couldn't spend it on candy as candy was rationed. My oldest brother and his friend cycled down from Glasgow, a 70 mile plus trip each way to visit me.

As I look back, despite the negatives and terrible war years, I realise what a personally enriching and learning experience my life in the country had been… in addition… so happy memories. I have returned often to visit Corrie and Lockerbie and I am forever known by the McCaughie family in a loving way as " The Evacuee". They are very proud to have a 70 plus Evacuee and a friendship of 60 plus years."

Jock Jardine lived at Heathfield near St Anns as a child during the war. He remembers that they first had a family evacuated from Glasgow - a young mother with her daughter, who was just a baby, and a niece, but they couldn't settle and left soon afterwards. It must have been difficult to live in such a quiet location after the hurly burly city.

However, much to John's delight they were then given two boys to billet. Looking like 2 lost sheep when they were picked up at Dinwoodie Station, Dick and Teddy Young from Glasgow were of a similar age so they were great company especially on the long trail to school - a 3mile bike ride and then the bus. Their teacher used to tell them off for their dirty muddy clogs. She told them to get them cleaned for next day and use some elbow grease. The next day they looked much the same and when the teacher asked why they were not cleaned one of the boys piped up with: "The elbow grease was done."

Everybody had to double up, but they just got on with it. **Drew Taylor's** father also had 2 boys whom he declared were so lousy so he put them in the bath with sheep dip!

Eastriggs received a contingent of Barnardo's boys from London. The large houses – **Stapleton Tower** owned by the Critchley family and **Springkell**, near Eaglesfield, owned by Sir Edward and Lady Johnson-Ferguson, became their homes for the duration of the war.

John Burgess moved house to Eastriggs, age 6, about the same time and remembered them with their uniform of navy jumpers and grey trousers and clogs! The boys attended Eastriggs and Annan schools. One boy, Frank Dickson remained at Stapleton until 1946. His memoir of his stay can be found in the "Devil's Porridge Exhibition" in Eastriggs. A whole class of pupils from Shawlands Academy in Glasgow were evacuated with their teacher, John Forrest, to Annan.

A Jewish boy, **Kurt Gutmann**, was evacuated to Annan, having escaped persecution in Nazi Germany. He was incredibly lucky because on Kristallnacht (The Night of Broken Glass - November 8th 1938 when Nazis attacked Jews and Jewish homes, shops and synagogues) his uncle was murdered, having been thrown out of a second floor window.

Kurt attended Annan Academy and when old enough enlisted in the Black Watch. After the war he returned to his home in Germany (then East Germany) and helped rebuild his country. He has been back to visit the Chalmers family with whom he lived so happily during the war.

Barnardos boys (from Devil's Porridge Exhibition)

CHAPTER 7
HOME GUARD

In May 1940 the Government announced that there should be a home front force to be called the Local Defence Volunteers. It would be formed by British subjects aged between 17 and 65. They were to have a uniform and weapons and were to serve for the duration of the war on a part time basis.

The impetus for this was the German invasion of Holland and Belgium by parachute troops disguised as Belgian or Dutch soldiers, clergymen and farm labourers. Their purpose was to create disorder and confusion and commit sabotage. Should the Germans land in Britain, then the country would have to be ready to defend itself.

In some parts of Scotland such as East Lothian, some of the LDV were further recruited into a secret sabotage corps. This also happened in Moffat. Just north of the burgh near Ruxton's Dump there is under a field a secret defence bunker which had been fitted out with a kitchen and a room with six iron beds. There was a chimney which stuck up through the ground, but was camouflaged and alongside lay several 50 gallon drums of oil fixed with detonators ready for a German convoy of trucks. After the war **Billy Duncan** found abandoned tins of butter and fruit cake.

It was not a "Dad's Army" - many of the volunteers and recruits were young. (My father, Drew Wilson was 22 and my Uncle George, only 21 when they joined in 1943.) They were farmers which was one of the reserved occupations. Others were blacksmiths or stonemasons or butchers and some were veterans of the First World War.

Home Guard Officers
Front row: 1,2,3,4,5, Bob Robinson, 7,Major Bell-Irving, Major Elliot, 10, -Campbell, Gray Moffat (Garvald)
2nd front 1,2, Bob Vernon, 4, Dr Sinclair, 6, -Kerr, 8,9, Jack Sheddan;
2nd back row1, 2, Adam Smith (Priestdykes), 4,5,6,7, Jim Copeland, Bill Irving, Jock McDougall, John Spence.

The No 2 Co. Dumfriesshire LDV was soon renamed the 1st Dumfriesshire Battalion Home Guard and was organised by Major - General Sir Eric S Girdwood, K.B.E.,C.B.,C.M.G. with his HQ at Moffat.

This battalion originally consisted of 4 platoons in the Moffat, Ecclefechan, Lockerbie and Kettleholm areas, but it was soon decided that the areas were too large and 5 separate companies were formed. These were as follows:-
Company 1 (A) under Major D Ralston (later Major VW Smith) covered the Moffat area;
Company 2 (B) under Major R Hope - Vere AFC (later Major JWS Galbraith) - the Lockerbie area;
Company 3 (C) under Major J Bell-Irving - the Kettleholm area ;
Company 4 (D) under Major W M Bell-MacDonald - the Lochmaben area and
Company 5 (E) under Major WD Elliot - the Eskdalemuir area.

Firstly, observation posts were established to cover road and rail and possible landing grounds. In June 1940 alone there were 25 road blocks and 6 observation points prepared and manned in this area. Equipment at first was non-existent. Boots and uniforms did not appear until September 1940. As many of the recruits were farmers, most had their own shotguns, but service rifles were so few that at first there was only one rifle for 10 men. Bizzarely 75 pikes were issued in Oct 1941, but held in reserve! By January 1942 more rifles were issued and the first of several machine guns. A year later Sten guns were provided.

The strength of the Battalion in June 1940 was 8 officers and 479 men, but by the end of November 1944 there were 47 officers (Home Guard commissions were introduced in 1941) and 834 men and 31 women. Compulsory enlistment was introduced in February 1942 to supplement numbers.

The Home Guard was a necessity. There was a real fear that the Germans would invade and in the darkest days of the war civilians could feel that there was some extra protection on the home front from the enemy.

It was not a "cushy" job either. The men were working long hours in their usual occupations to provide the food and milk needed in those days of rationing and torpedoing of merchant ships. Some were providing vital services for the nation as well as training two to three times a week and Sundays. Live ammunition was used and there were fatalities in the area in the course of duty - Major T C Graham DCM and Private A McQueen.

Dad, George and their cousin Ronnie Carmichael of Lochbank Farm, were all in the Lochmaben Home Guard. Dad never talked about it much, but he did say he learned to shoot whilst training at Corncockle Quarry near Templand and one of their tasks was to sit on the roof of Lochmaben Church to watch out for enemy aircraft. They are photographed here in front of Lochmaben Primary School some with other members of the Lochmaben Home Guard were James McGhie (Lieutenant-2 in charge), JH McQueen, AA Smith, J Davidson, RS Greirson, Willie Mair and D F Robertson.

Lochmaben Home Guard

Jack Maxwell's family farmed at The Gall, Boreland. His father was in the Observer Corps and he and his brother were in the Boreland Home Guard. They had to spend three days a week practising and out on patrol once a fortnight. These were night and day exercises with the men from the regular army teaching them. Jack told me about one day which could have ended in a complete disaster.

There was an old WW1 bunker at Slodahill where they were being trained to throw grenades. They had to come out one at a time and throw the bomb over the wall of a courtyard. They had to stand up on the step to see over and then throw the bomb, then duck, but unfortunately someone's grenade hit the wall near the animals' cubicles and it bounced back! Luckily a quick thinking regular soldier kicked the grenade away before it exploded. The soldier, a **Sergeant Smith**, was very badly hurt in the leg, but he saved their lives. (Later awarded the BEM for gallantry).

Boreland Home Guard met in the school where they had lectures. Jack remembered one scenario which had Lockerbie as a German target. The men were told not to fight, but to retreat. The commander said, "Retreat past the church and reassemble at Fauld Wood".

One chap from Gillesbie, shouted out, " That might be difficult. The wood has retreated before us". They'd cut down that wood in WW1 and the commander had been using an old map.

Being in the Guard was dangerous because live ammunition was used. Jack was once in charge of a machine gun firing tracer bullets up the hill while the rest of the troops had to crawl up under this fire.

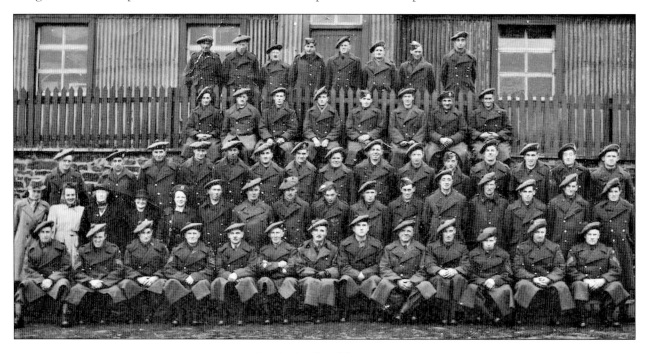

Corrie and Boreland and Eskdalemuir Home Guard
Front row left to right: 1,2,3,Frank Carruthers,5,6, Major Elliot, Gray Moffat, Bill Irving, Jim Copeland, 11, Willie Bell, Eben Irving.
2nd row: 1, Peggy McDougall, 3, 4, 5, 6, Jack McDougall, 8, 9, 10, 11, 12, Jack Maxwell, 14, 15, 16;
3rd row: 1.2. –White, Jim Laurie, Bob Lynn, Robert Black, 7, Frank Duff, 9, 10, 11, Bobby Rae, Sandie Fleming, 14, Charlie Graham;
4th row: 1, 2, Tom Maxwell, Jim McGaughie, 5, Tom Laurie, Jim Harkness, Tom Burnie,;
Back row: Kit Oliver, Dick Petson, Jock Little, 4, Malcolm Maxwell, 6, -Duff, 8.

Tom Laurie remembered that when the Home Guard started they were not given proper supplies and they only had sticks - no guns until later when they received American rifles and had bayonet training. They were supplied with armbands and eventually they got a uniform along with a great coat which they were allowed to keep along with the gaiters to prevent tics. They trained twice a week and on Sundays. Regular soldiers taught them how to break necks and arms or if the enemy was coming towards you, how to break knees.

It must have been quite a commitment for some farmers who would still have the milking to do twice a day every day as well as the other essential farm tasks of producing food.

Alec Smith recalled that some of their farm workers were also in the Guard and one day they had orders to "take" Priestdykes. One of the men remarked that it would be easy because they knew the farm layout, however the officers had booby trapped all the yard with trip wire. They all fell over!

Jock Jardine from Heathfield was a member of the Home Guard for one month before the Guard was stood down! He had just been issued with his uniform and a great coat, but was allowed to keep them and made great use of them in winter when driving tractors as this was before tractors had cabs. He was in the cadets as a youngster and worked alongside the Home Guard, meeting in the shed on the Estate yard and skivvying for the elders. His uncle, Henry Jardine was a veteran of WW1 and he was the squadron leader.

St Mungo Home Guard Platoon
Front row:- Gregor MacAdam, Jim Campbell, Peter Donaldson, John Kerr (Nutholmshaw), David Campbell, Major Bell-Irving, Willie Read, Wilson Fraser, John McPherson, Michael Reid (Bengall), Bob Dalgleish;
2nd row:- Jim Scott (Broom), Joe Irving, Jim Shanks, David Lockhart (Pilmuir), Frank Beattie, ?, Johnnie Rogerson, Willie Johnstone;
3rd row:- George Patterson, Archie Williamson, David Galloway, Ted Sandbach (Groom), Bob Drummond, - Shannon (Brocklebank), George Patterson
4th row:- Bill Hunter, Jimmy Martin, Bobby Huntingdon, David Coates, Kit Grierson;
5th (back row):- Tom Johnstone, Bobby Shanks, Jack Taylor (Bengall).

Andrew Spence of Corrielaw recalled his time in the Home Guard.

"In 1940 I joined the Home Guard and trained at Kettleholm Hall. In 1941 we had a 500 cc Ariel motorbike on the farm. It was a useful addition as it had a good petrol allowance and if one of us was using the bike, the car was still available. The Sergeant Major called Smith gave me the post of despatch rider. He was very well respected in the platoon as he instilled confidence and respect through his encouragement.

One Sunday we were having 303 rifle practice near Ecclefechan at Brown Moor targets. The officers found that they had forgotten glue and I was despatched to find a substitute. Horsburghs was a big grocer's shop and I went to the back door and asked for flour to mix with water. They were very pleasant about it and did not charge for the flour.

I had always enjoyed using an air gun and at the next meeting, I was parking the motorbike when Sergeant Major Smith came to speak to me about the previous target practice. He asked me what experience I had with a rifle and I said that was the first time I had fired one. He said, "Did you realise that you had the best score of any others that day?" Whether it was strictly true or not, he was the officer who liked to praise and encourage one.

We were very saddened when a year or so later Smith was badly injured with a hand grenade exploding in a trench. Many Eskdalemuir men would have been killed if he had not risked his life throwing it away.

(Read Jack Maxwell's account of this).

There was a very real threat of invasion in 1943-44 and my friend, Cassels Little, and I were transferred to the Signals Department. We had to man the telephone in the drill hall. We were instructed by one Sergeant Conway who was also an electric engineer. We had to work all day at hay or whatever, until 8.30 and then travel to the drill hall and spend the night at the telephone. This was the time when we were working long hours on the farm and I was not good at standing still, owing to having hurt my back at the age of 14. That night we were having a lecture on dismantling the 303 rifle. There were about 12 of us under one Sergeant Reid who was a carpenter in charge of the electric lighting at Castlemilk. Well I felt very faint after only 5 minutes and asked if I could sit down. My face must have been very white because the others soon rushed a chair towards me."

Emilio Dicerbo told me the story of one very excitable Moffat lad. There was a 2-day exercise whereby the Home Guard were to hold Moffat against the Battle School (see chp on Home life) who were to "attack" the town. Kids with bikes were recruited to carry messages between the opposing sides.

One day this lad was sent to deliver a message to the old Police Station from an outpost on the Selkirk Road. The boy came racing down the hill on his bike when a soldier threw a thunderflash at him. This unnerved him – the bike went one way and he sailed over the wall into a field.

Later when he eventually reached the police station without his trousers, the officer asked him where his trousers were. He replied, "They're ower the wa' and fu' o' keech!"

Moffat Home Guard
Left to right
Back row:- ? McRobert, T Burgess, J Wilson, ? Whitby, D Johnstone, R Bruce, J Graham
Middle row:- R Johnstone, ? Routledge, J Dalgleish, T Boyes, W Sharpe, J Burnett, A Porteuos, B Johnstone
Front row:- A Forson, T Murray, W Currie, W Halliday, I Lockhart, V Smith, W Mackie, J McIlwraith, A Bruce, T Fortune, W Johnstone.

Lochmaben HG -Platoon
Back row l-r: James McGhie, E Mundel, E Mair, William Smith, Crawford Smith
Front row: ?, G Mundel, Tommy Telfer

Annan Home Guard

In 1944 it became apparent that an invasion of Europe would take place and consequently it was difficult to convince the men of the Home Guard that they were still needed. The officers decided to work them even harder according to Hope-Vere, but towards the end of the year there was talk and then the reality of disbanding the Guard. There had been 1,727,095 members of the British Home Guard. 1,206 of them were killed on duty or died of their wounds.

CHAPTER 8
FARM LIFE

Due to Britain being an island and not self sufficient in foodstuffs, the war time Government had to take more direct control over farmers' lives and issue a series of directives so that the country might produce more foodstuffs and become less reliant on overseas' supplies. A move in this direction was the 1940 National Farm Survey.

Nothing like this had been attempted since the Domesday Book in 1087. Every holding of more than 5 acres was to be surveyed by retired farmers and volunteer committees. It would take into account not only the qualities of the land, but also the qualities of the farmer; the state of the land and buildings; the types of soil, the acreage of crops and grasslands as well as the extent of infestations of rabbits and rats. This survey led to the production of detailed maps with over 300,000 farms being recorded. The countryside and its resources were then to be mobilised more efficiently for the war effort.

The UK population was around 48 milllion then and only about 1 million were engaged in agriculture so much of our food was imported. It would be necessary in the event of blockade for more land to be brought under cultivation so in the first winter of the war in 1939-40 over 2 million acres were to ploughed up.

This was no easy task as men had been called into the forces and there was also a shortage of ploughs and horses and tractors. In some cases ploughing took place by moonlight or with specially attached lights so the farmer could meet the deadline - and it was no easy task as this was one of the hardest winters with heavy frosts. **Jack Maxwell**, from the Gall, remembered it well. His sister's birthday occurred in winter and the family had friends from Cumberland staying for the party. From the Friday night to the following Tuesday they were snowed up and couldn't get home, but neither could the Maxwells get their milk to the dairy. Nevertheless eventually it took two horse wagons to take the delayed milk churns to the train at Lockerbie.

War did bring some mechanisation to the farms:- In 1939 the UK had 55,000 tractors but by 1945 it had 175,000.

Alec Smith remembers the yellow Fordson Tractor they used. The family had to help plough up the land at West Acres in Lockerbie, and they were told what to plant. At Priestdykes at threshing time, the Patties of Hightae brought the threshing mill and bailer and even a hut for the workers to stay in until the harvest was done. The farmers got extra rations for the mill workers.

Double summertime was introduced to allow farmers more daylight working.

This Fordson came from the USA shortly after the war on the Lend- Lease scheme. One of the men planting the tatties is John Mundell recently returned from POW camp, Alex Smith is driving the tractor.

The Ministry of Food guaranteed that all children under the age of 5 and all expectant mothers were to receive a pint of milk a day so milk production also had to increase. The local newspapers carrying adverts exhorting the dairy farmers to do their best, also recorded farmers' grievances about the price they were getting for milk. It had gone down from 1s 5d in January 1940 to 1s 3d in the February, despite the fact that the cost of feedstuffs had increased by about 50 %. The farmers hoped that the Milk Marketing Board would press upon the Government that the price was inadequate. (This is the same story today).

For the first time in this country AI (artificial insemination) was used for cattle to ensure a strong, healthy and productive herd and grass was cut to be used as silage for winter fodder.

In the farm dairies, milk cans were steamed for cleaning and the milk was cooled over pipes which looked a bit like old fashioned wash boards. The milk was then put into churns - or bottles on the farms. Sometimes the dairyman went around the villages with the milk for sale to be ladled into the folks' own jugs.

In the South West because of poor communications, the dairy farmer had to turn a lot of his milk into cheese so that he could at least get some fresh produce to a market.

Sheep were less important, but Alec Smith remembered the day in Lockerbie when he was herding 400 January tups along Sydney Place, down Bridge Street and onto the High Street when one saw its reflection in the glass door of Henderson's, the Saddlers, and charged into it.

Drew Taylor from Lochwood Mains recalled that keeping a pig was encouraged and the "Killing Day" was a great social occasion with all the kids eyeing the pork bones enviously.

Another Government directive concerned vermin. Rats in particular were targeted as a pair of rats can multiply and produce 880 offspring. They could wreak havoc especially at harvest time so it was often the job for land girls to put down the poison and collect the dead animals. Shooting rabbits was a regular task to prevent them eating the new shoots, but they also provided cheap meat for stews and pies and folk could make a penny or two. Drew told me that rabbits were sent from Wamphray in special hampers down to Leeds for the Black Market.

During World War Two much of the work on farms was still manual and farmers needed all the help they could get. Many employees had been enlisted in the forces and the farmers themselves had Home Guard duties.

The photo here was taken on a farm near Lochmaben in 1943 showing the men at their break in the hay cutting. Note the use of horses.

Far from being quiet places of respite from the noise of the towns which had to put up with army manoeuvres, lorries and jeeps and troops on and off duty, the farms of Annandale suddenly became heavily populated hives of activity with the arrival of large numbers of land girls, POWs, evacuees and soldiers.

Esbie Harvest.

To help the farming communities, the Government introduced new measures. Women were recruited into the Land Army and children were allowed time off school (crucially at tattie picking time). Farmers were allowed to queue up at the local schools to seek as many as 30 children for each farm to help gather this harvest. Even more welcome on the farms were the prisoners of war. They were deemed to be of no danger to the local communities as most of them had been farmers themselves before being conscripted into the enemy forces.

In this photograph left to right are: Fritz Wingerath, Robert Shultz, ?, Mr Kennedy from Cumrue, George Wilson, Drew Wilson and Otto.

One other aspect of farm life during the war was the regular use of farms by the army for manoeuvres or for practising shooting. This led to major disruptions as well as sometimes the loss of animal lives. **Jack Jardine** remembers trying to take cattle for grazing from the farm at Heathfield, St Anns to the Barony - a journey of about 11 miles. They ended up having to take them about 3 o'clock in the morning because there were so many convoys of lorries moving soldiers from site to site - Edinburgh to Yorkshire often 2-300 lorries- imagine getting the cattle mixed up with those! They were often out in the fields ploughing with the horses when whole battalions of men on parade came marching single file across the field.

Jack Maxwell's farm at the Gall was regularly used by the army every three or four days - sometimes without warning. They would be firing into the next hill so often that they had to take chances with their sheep and there were a few near scrapes with 'friendly fire'. Once Jack was ploughing turnips with horses when he was "caught" in the firing line. They told him later that they were firing guns as a communication device to get him off the hill!

Bill Gibson remembers that at Thorniethwaite Farm some of the land was used by the army to train despatch riders on motorbikes as well as practising with bren guns.

Tom Laurie's family farm, Carterton, on the Castlemilk Estate was heavily used for bombing practice. Huge 25 pounders really shook up the farm, made the house shudder and damaged the fields. After the war they had to be careful when putting in fencing in case there were unexploded bombs lying in the deep peat. 150 ewes were killed on the farm. Tom said they got little warning when the army were coming. He thinks they were practising artillery firing for the campaign in North Africa.

Tom also recalls seeing the German planes heading for Clydebank and flying low over the farm to avoid the radar.

One moonlight night in 1943 Jack Jardine was awakened around 3am thinking he'd heard the milk lorry crash into the end of the house. He got up to see enemy planes flying over Lochpark near St Anns heading for Clydebank. One of them must have seen the greenhouse reflecting light and dropped a bomb. It landed at Kirkbank Farm with a huge piece of shrapnel cutting right through an old oak tree!

DAIRY FARMERS

The Nation depends on YOU
For

WINTER MILK

You have done a splendid war-time job—but still greater effort is required.

The Nation must be kept fit and well — and NEXT winter's milk must be planned for now.

> EVERY HEIFER CALVING NEXT AUTUMN WILL PROVIDE A DAILY MILK SUPPLY FOR 25 YOUNG CHILDREN DURING THE COLD, BLACK - OUT MONTHS

And remember that all classes of consumers look to you for increased supplies during the winter of 1943-44.

MAKE YOUR ARRANGEMENTS NOW!

ISSUED BY THE DEPARTMENT OF AGRICULTURE FOR SCOTLAND

(Annandale Herald and Record)

CHAPTER 9
PRISONERS OF WAR, THE BARONY AND HALLMUIR

During the war there were five Prisoner of War Camps established in Dumfriesshire. One of the largest was in Annandale on the estate known as the Barony (at Parkgate) owned since 1919 by the Galbraith family. Unlike many great houses in the area, the Barony House was not demolished after the war and nowadays is home to the Agricultural College.

Present Day Barony.

In 1939 the whole estate was taken over by the army and a Jewish "pioneer" Corps built the huts which were used firstly for army training, then later as accommodation for prisoners from Italy, Germany, Austria and several other "alien" nations.

The camp stood on two sides of the road and was officially known as both Camp 182 and Camp 298. In May 1945 Mr Bieri on behalf of the Red Cross inspected Camp 182. (The management of POW Camps had to follow strict internationally agreed rules.) At that time there was a total of 1968 prisoners of which 1821 were German and 124 Ukrainians, some French, Austrians, Czechs, Rumanians and Hungarians. The chief Camp leader was Barthal Giesen.

In his report, Mr Bieri described the camp as being one used for German prisoners, but before 1944 it had been used as a transit camp for Italians. "Each compound was surrounded by barbed wire and lay in a beautiful park. There were lovely old trees and two nice lakes in which bathing was permitted. The POWs had made a little boat for rowing and there was ample room for exercise. It seemed in some places to look more like a recreation camp than a POW camp. One of the best camps we have ever seen."

Many of the POWs had worked hard making improvements with paths and flowerbeds. The inspector noted that the camp had electric light and stove heating; had sufficient sanitary installations and each man had a blanket and sleeping bag. There were no complaints about the food and a sample menu would be porridge for breakfast; liver and boiled potatoes for dinner and bread, margarine and sausage for supper.

A British dentist visited every week and there was a camp infirmary with German medical officers and sufficient medical supplies. There were no contagious diseases and no serious cases bar 1 case of concussion and 8 cases of severe under nourishment. (Some POWs had recently come from a camp in Jersey where there had been very few rations.)

Most of the men had their own uniforms and the majority of the POWs worked on agricultural jobs with a general rate of pay of 1½ d an hour. (The POWs had to buy their own cigarettes, coffee and writing paper.)

There was a Protestant (German) chaplain, but a Swiss chaplain came into the camp from a nearby church from time to time to take the RC Mass. There were also educational classes of which English was the most popular. The POWs had organised themselves into a male voice choir, and there was a vocal quartet. They had a few musical instruments of which 6 were home made mandolins. A loudspeaker relayed radio and although there was a cinema (in Cinema Field) it was too expensive to get films. POWs received letters and parcels including several from the German Red Cross. Many of the POWs thought that the foodstuffs should be kept in Germany for the benefit of their wives and children and not sent to England to men " who are well fed and not hungry".

The general impression was of beautiful surroundings and good management. "The main wish of the POWs (excepting of course "news from home") was to be able to stay in the camp until they are set at liberty."

Barony Lakes.

Most of the Germans had been captured since D-Day. These prisoners were "graded by their politics" by the military authorities and therefore there were no hard line Nazis at the Barony. (Nazis were graded "black", other Germans being either grey or white. Those graded "white " were deemed to be trusted to work outside the camp without guards).

Dumfriesshire had more camps than any other county in Scotland which correlated well with it being an arable agricultural district needing a high percentage of agricultural workers, but German workers were still employed on farms three years after the cessation of hostilities. This provoked an outcry from some people who talked about the unethical use of "serf labour", but what must also be remembered was the slow move to demob British army personnel and there was still rationing. The farms still needed workers. More than 25,000 of the German POWs "elected to stay in Britain."

Book Cover.

Dumfries - Burns' Statue

The POWs produced several newsletters written partly in German and partly in English which contained beautiful linocuts. A book of drawings has also been left behind and is now in the Barony Library.

Some of the prisoners made toys to sell to the locals. Illustrated here is a drawing made by S G Hesse satirising this transaction. **John Knipe** remembers the toys - they were made of wood - a hen on a stick with a piece of twine. You had to squeeze the string and the hen would peck at the ground.

John Knipe and **Tony Walker** both remember seeing a huge model of Cologne Cathedral built in Cinema Field. Sadly it was destroyed and there seems to be no extant photograph.

Alfred Bojanitz was born in Germany of Jugoslav/ Serbian immigrant parents. He was conscripted into the Wehrmacht in

Black Market

1940 and then captured and sent to the Barony and then later to South Devon. His daughter, Maria, has written a book about her father, "Alfred the Great", and in it mentions several of his friends from the Barony. She told me that Arnold Becker was a POW at the Barony from 1944-47 and was a ration store man in one of the camp's cookhouses; Franz Debeuser was in the mandolin concert band; Fritz Ebert (1944-46) worked on farms and the forestry and Wilhelm Freise played in the 1947 football team. When he returned to Germany in 1947 he became Professor of Nordische Philologie in Lubingen.

Gordon Kerr was stationed at the Barony shortly after the war. Here he has written his own account of what life was like for both soldiers and prisoners:-

"In April 1946, at the age of eighteen, I was drafted into the British army and after several months of infantry training was posted to 298 Prisoner of war camp, the Barony, Parkgate, Dumfriesshire.

I arrived at the camp by way of the local bus which deposited me and my kit outside Parkgate post office. It was a pleasant Autumn afternoon and I was impressed by the beauty of the locality. Getting directions from the post office I climbed the style over the dyke and could immediately see the camp stretching out before me. This conformed to all the standards I was led to expect from seeing films of wartime exploits involving escapes from prison camps. There was a tall barbed wire enclosing the area, with guard towers every hundred yards, and powerful flood lights on tall poles to illuminate the area after dark. However as I got nearer, I could see that the guard towers were unmanned, no machine guns mounted and even more surprising, the first person I encountered was a prisoner of war walking towards me on the outside of the wire!! As I could speak a few words of German, learned at school, we greeted each other and he pointed me towards Barony House, which was to be my residence and workplace for the next eighteen months.

I was billeted in what had previously been the servants' wing, sharing a room with three other soldiers and my workplace was in the orderly room, which I suspect was a drawing room in a previous era, where I carried out administrative duties. First, I was introduced to the Commandant, a colonel in the Royal Artillery, who welcomed me to the unit and gave me a short 'pep' talk on his expectations of me. He went on to stress the importance of how the prisoners should always be treated in a fair and respectful manner, the wisdom of which soon became apparent to me. Secondly, I met my immediate boss, Sergeant Burgoyne, a young career soldier who ran the orderly room, and he explained what my duties would be. The logistics of running a camp containing some eight thousand inmates and a staff of some forty British ranks was always a problem, and there was an endless array of forms, requisitions, movement orders to be completed on a daily basis to keep operation moving, so there was no

Postcard of Barony POWS.

shortage of work. The disparity in numbers between British staff and prisoners is obvious, so the Commandant's strictures on the treatment of prisoners made a lot of sense.

Until this time, my experience in the Army had been limited to barrack life where everything was highly structured and disciplined, there was a drill for everything, all done by numbers, you marched in platoon formation to meals, arms drill, foot drill, field exercises, inspections etc., etc. Buttons, badges, buckles and boots all highly polished, and web equipment pipeclayed to perfection. This unit was totally different, no parades, no drills and as long as you were clean, tidy and shaven, the spit and polish of infantry units was not an issue. This transition came as a shock at first but was easy to adapt to.

The prisoners of war were clad in coats, tunics and trousers of wool serge dyed to dark bluish grey colour, each garment being emblazoned with a dark red diamond on the back of the tunic and coat , and on the right leg of the trousers. This outfit was topped off by a cloth cap with a skip similar to a baseball cap. Boots, socks, underwear was standard British army issue. So they were reasonably clad for the climate. It was prohibited for them to display badges of rank, decorations or unit insignia on their clothing.

All the POWs at Barony camp were non-commissioned ranks of the German army with a few naval personnel thrown in. They had all been subjected to screening processes known as de-nazification which had weeded out the hard core Nazis and known war criminals, who were detained in a different sort of camp in the Shetlands.

The Barony was a working camp, which meant that the army would hire out labour to local farmers and foresters, etc. - the revenue of which would defray some of the costs of running the camp. There was a trickle - down effect for the POW'S too, they got 'paid' in vouchers (Lagergeld) which they could redeem in the compound canteen for small luxuries. They could even qualify for a bonus if they worked over a certain amount of hours in the week. This bonus was paid in cigarettes, which was the real currency inside the wire. A proportion of a POW's earnings was diverted to a credit account which would be returned to him on repatriation, so that he would have some assets to draw on. This arrangement seemed to work reasonably well for the farmers and POW alike.

The camp compound was self-governing and was controlled by the Lagerfuhrer (Camp leader) who was appointed by the Commandant. It was his responsibility to maintain order in the compound and he had a staff of appointees to assist him in this task. As could be expected, minor offences did occur inside the compound and these were dealt with by the Commandant who administered summary justice although it was paradoxical to imprison a prisoner. By and large this system worked quite well and I cannot recall any incident of major concern.

One could ask why the government in late 1946, more than a year after hostilities concluded in Europe did not decree that all war prisoners should be returned to their homeland. The answer is manifold. Large areas of Western Europe were in ruins, there was no accommodation for a sudden influx of thousands of returning combatants. Food and fuel shortages were endemic, that coupled with the hundreds of thousands of 'displaced persons' who were already scattered in camps across Western Europe, it was too great a problem for the government to adopt this solution. The better option was to maintain the camps in Britain and to affect a controlled release as and when circumstances allowed. This explains why the camps existed well into 1948.

As for the prisoners of war, my observation was that they all accepted this situation and were resigned to fact that they would be detained for an indeterminate time, but were prepared to make the best of the situation and sit it out. This could explain why none of the POWs ever attempted to escape. They were clad, fed and housed and were probably grateful that they had survived the war.

A significant number of the POWs could speak English, some with a distinct American accent, which was explained by them being captured by American forces in North Africa, Italy, and other theatres of war, which led to internment in U.S.A. and Canada where they learned the language. Communication between these prisoners and the British personnel was easy so many dialogues developed, with exchange of views on a multitude of subjects, after all, both sides were trying to pass the time!

The day to day running of the camp depended heavily on POW labour, cooking, cleaning, clerical work, driving pool, general maintenance were tasks carried out by the internees, who, in return were paid at the same scale as the agricultural workers. The rank and file cookhouse was situated at the south end of the camp and was run by two German cooks and one waiter (who didn't speak English - so complaining to him didn't achieve much). The fare they produced from standard army rations was surprisingly good and compared well with food provided at other military establishments. I seem to recall that meat loaf was a staple, as was the cowboy breakfast, two rashers of bacon and a dollop of beans, which was a good start to the day.

Summer time in the camp was quite pleasant as outdoor activities could be enjoyed for both POWs and staff alike, games of football, walks etc. Adjacent to Barony house at that time was a large ornamental pond, which was actually inside the compound, and this was used as a swimming pool by both sides. During duck season decoy ducks could be seen floating on the pond, placed there by the Commandant. His office overlooked the pond and he could be seen occasionally rushing outside clutching his 12 bore shotgun. I don't think the mallards were in any great danger as duck never appeared on the menu.

Winter could be a different matter altogether as trying to keep warm was a priority for everyone. Fuel was in extremely short supply and was strictly rationed - one bucket of coal a week per room. This meant you could enjoy a good fire for one night and freeze for six days. This was compounded by the electrical supply to Barony house, which like many country houses of its time, had a generator which provided power of a sort, probably in the 12 volt d.c. range, which was no use for heating purposes. However, it was found that that the circuit to the compound perimeter floodlights was still live and was connected to the local 240 volt supply. Some hundred yards of cable was acquired and teed into the supply and then terminated, strangely enough, in our bedroom in the servants wing. This allowed us to plug in a one bar electric fire, which gave an impression of warmth, but more importantly, allowed us the use of a radio so we could listen to programs on the Home and Forces BBC bands, and also AFN (American Forces network from Germany) and Radio Eireann.

The winters of 1946/47 and 1947/48 were severe, very cold and frequent snow storms. After one particular storm, the road from Moffat to Dumfries was completely blocked to traffic, which meant our convoys of trucks could not deliver our labour units to the farms. However, we did have a workforce of some six thousand, so they were set to clear the roads, which was done in one day much to the relief of the local community.

There was one dark chapter in the history of the camp. Sometime in mid 1947 we received orders from Scottish Command in Edinburgh that we would be required to accommodate some 800 prisoners of war who were in transit, by sea, from Italy. These prisoners were of Ukrainian origin, who had sided with the invading German armies in Russia, as they regarded them as liberators who would free them from the oppression of the Soviets. It was recommended that these prisoners should be segregated from the main camp, and so a satellite camp was set up in Hallmuir, Dumfriesshire, to house them. The POWs finally arrived and they were duly clad, fed and housed without any major problem. The language difference was a major stumbling block as Ukrainian interpreters were extremely scarce. However it was found that most of these POWs had a working knowledge of German, so that a dialogue of some kind could be carried on. The compilation of camp records was a bit of a headache for the staff as most of their names appeared to be a random jumble of consonants.

By and large, the Ukrainians turned out to be a fairly amiable bunch and were popular in the local community. There is one surviving relic of their stay in Hallmuir, which is the camp chapel which was a standard army hut, but decorated inside to simulate an orthodox Ukrainian church with murals and icons, all painted by the detainees, some of whom had distinct artistic talents. This chapel is well worth a visit.

It could have been in early 1948 when we received orders that the Ukrainian POWs were to be repatriated to the U.S.S.R. . The British government decreed that every POW should be given the opportunity to stay in Britain and be assimilated into the local community and a number of the wiser prisoners availed themselves of this offer. The remainder of the prisoners were duly shipped out to Odessa, in the Crimea where on disembarkation they were promptly arrested, deemed to be traitors of the Soviet Union, and executed.

Ukrainian Chapel.

It took some weeks for news of this savage event to filter back to Barony Camp, much to the horror of staff and prisoner alike. Everyone associated with this event had a sense of guilt at being part of the process which led to this horrible ending.

In the Spring of 1948 it was obvious that the repatriation of prisoners was accelerating and the camp would soon close. I was not able to witness this event as in May my long awaited demobilization papers arrived and I was able to bid farewell to my friends, both British and German, and return to civilian life.

One item on display sticks in my memory. This was a model railway layout which one of the POWs had assembled for this event. There were yards of track, several locomotives and all kinds of rolling stock many hand crafted from scrap metal. The whole thing was powered by electricity, and it actually worked! The owner must have been a total model railway 'freak' to have lugged all this stuff halfway across Europe to end up in a POW camp in Scotland!.

Another odd item which surfaced was a massive typewriter, probably about 30 lbs. in weight, and the POW who had it in his possession couldn't type!. The typewriter defeated us too, as the typeface and keyboard were in the Cyrillic alphabet!. We assumed that this machine was a souvenir from the Russian front."

What follows are some personal stories of men who had been prisoners of war at The Barony, Parkgate and at Hallmuir, Lockerbie.

Erich Schwartz

Erich Schwartz who came to work on the Taylor's farm at Lochwood Mains was a top grade footballer. The parish held its summer league football which was organised by a Nethermill goalie and POWs were not supposed to play in the teams, but Erich was too good a player to be watching from the sidelines. He was given a position and told to stay quiet and all would be well. However during the game an altercation with an opposing player revealed that he was a German too!

The POWs at first were brought under guard to the farms, but later Erich lived at Lochwood Mains, as part of the family, for 5 days at a time before returning to the camp. He desperately wanted to learn English so young Drew Taylor tried to "help" him. There was some hilarity when he used to get the names of body parts muddled.

Erich had lived in what was East Germany and wanted to return because he had a sweetheart in Kreiz, but it was some time after the war had ended that Erich managed to get back home. Then the country had become Communist and communication with the west became difficult for Erich who had been corresponding with Drew's mother. He did, however, send her this wooden "plate".

Plate from Erich.

Bernhard Reetz

Bernhard was born in 1921 into a farming family in Dobberphul, Germany. This town was in Pomerania, Prussia, in the North East, but after the war became part of Poland. Bernhard had 3 brothers and 2 sisters. His eldest brother was killed in the war.

The family think Bernhard was conscripted into the German army and served for a time as a Corporal. Towards the end of the war, he and his colleagues had to cross the River Elbe. He didn't know then that there would be Americans waiting for them on the other side. The Americans beat them back, but then they were pursued by the Russian army. They surrendered to the Russians and Bernard would not see his family again for 10 years.

He was first taken to a prisoner of war camp in Belgium and then in 1946 was taken to Leicester and then moved to the Barony POW camp (or EVW Hostel as it was then called) at Parkgate, Lochmaben. From there he was sent out to work on the local farms. He eventually lodged in the bothy at Lochbrow Farm.

Bernhard did not wish to go back home and elected to stay in Dumfriesshire, but even in the late 1950s police would come to his door to check up on him and see if he was at the same address. His card was stamped for the last time in1961 and this made him finally exempt from registration with the police.

Although Bernhard was working fairly close by at Lochbrow Farm, he didn't meet his future wife, **Dorothy Callendar** who lived at Mossvale, Lochmaben, until 1949 in Blackpool! Dorothy told me the story that she and her friend had got the chance of two seats on a bus trip to Blackpool organised by the Germans. They met on the beach. Later they met again at a dance in Lockerbie Town Hall.

Bernard.

They married in Balcastle Hotel in 1954 having saved hard for a honeymoon that would take them to meet Bernhard's family.

His father, unfortunately had died, but Dorothy was able to meet her German in laws and was made part of the family. Bernhard's family had tried to move away during the war to escape the Russians. They walked for nearly a week and thought they were safe when they reached Rugen (Germany). They stayed there where they lived in a one bedroom flat in a huge house which had been divided up. It became part of East Germany after the war.

Dorothy and Bernhard were happily married for 53 years and had two children, but sadly Bernhard died in 2007. Dorothy told me that he loved meeting people and when on many of their caravanning holidays if people asked what nationality he was, he always said, "I'm Scottish"!

Gunter Naumaun

Gunter was brought from the Barony to work at Esbie Farm along with several other POWs. One, **Robert Shultz** is pictured on page 108 here on the farm with my late father, **Drew Wilson** and the collie, Roy. They lived in the bothy which is a substantial building consisting of two rooms each with a fireplace.

Everyone seemed to have been on very good terms with one another. My late Aunt went out to Dusseldorf and Cologne in the 1950s on a holiday staying with the family of another POW, **Fritz Wingerath**. The family still own a lovely wooden box made by one of the German POWs. There also exists an oil painting done by an Italian POW. It

Gunter.

seems to be a view of Pistoia. I remember my father telling me that he had learned one word of Italian - "mangiare" - he heard it everyday - it means "to eat"!

Esbie POWs

Wingerath Factory

Aunt May & Ingleborg Wingerath   *Aunt May & AnnieMay Naumann*

Robert, Roy and Drew Wilson

Mrs Laurie (**nee Common** from Crossdykes Farm) showed me a beautiful jewellery box made for her family by Italians from the Kirkpatrick Fleming Camp and a cigarette lighter made by **Reno Pentori**, who kept in touch over the years. At Crossdykes there were two Italians from Sicily. They also made baskets (from willow wands) one of which Mrs Laurie still uses for fruit.

Painting of Pistoia by an Italian POW.

Box. made by Italian POW

Bill Gibson remembered two Italian POWs who were cousins and came from Palermo - **Angelo Valente** and **Guiseppe (Joe) Landolini**. They lived in the bothy at Thorniethwaite Farm where Mrs Gibson gave them their meals. The family thought it was funny that the Italians ate their sweet before their main course. When the war ended the men were told by the authoriies that they had only two hours to pack. Joe cried because he had no time to say goodbye to all his friends in Lochmaben.

Michael Kacedan

I spoke to **Peggy Richardson** from Lochmaben who married Michael Kacedan who was a Ukranian prisoner of war at Hallmuir Camp. This is what she told me.

"Michael was born on 12th April 1925 in a little village called Dubrawka, Stryj in West Ukraine. The nearest big city was Lvov. His parents eked a life out of the land, growing what they could for their family and taking the surplus to the shops in exchange for essentials such as paraffin. It was a hard life and there was little chance of a good education.

The last time Michael saw his parents (Anton and Marie); sister and younger brothers was when he was 16 years old.

In 1941 the Russian Red Army came into the Ukraine. Michael along with other young boys and some of the younger men went underground, but hey had sealed their fate because now they could not go home. They were terrified that if they returned and were caught by the Russians they would be shot as partisans.

They joined up with the Ukranian army and hoped to meet either the US or British forces. They eventually met the British in Italy.

From Italy they were sent to Britain and landed up in Edinburgh and then were brought down to Hallmuir Camp outside Lockerbie which had just been vacated by Italian prisoners of war in 1947.

After the war Stalin asked for them back enticing them with promises that all would be well. Some unfortunately trusted Stalin only to be shot on arrival in Russian territory. Michael chose well - he stayed.

For some time he worked on various farms around the neighbourhood, but he was desperate to make a real life for himself and so asked permission to leave. He got digs with Mrs Studholme in Lockerbie and began working with McColl Wells and helped build some new houses in Lockerbie. In 1948/9 The Red Cross contacted Michael and he learned through them that his sister, Anna, had been looking for him. They were at last able to exchange letters.

Michael met Peggy at a dance in Lockerbie Town Hall and a few years later they married. They brought up a family together, but sadly, Michael died in 1986.

Michael Kacedan

Peggy has travelled twice to the Ukraine to visit her in-laws. She learned that the Russians had taken away Michael's two brothers to be educated, leaving his sister to help the parents. The one good thing that resulted from this was the excellent education that the boys had which allowed them to became school teachers."

Chapter 10
End of the War

Relief was felt by all when the end of the war in Europe was announced in May 1945 and again in August when victory over Japan was declared. Many of the forces, however, were still awaiting demob and return from abroad. Some were to wait until late 1946!

I am grateful to Eric Watson who sent me this copy of a photograph of the signing of the peace treaty at Rheims. In the photograph are British, American, Russian and French generals witnessing the surrender of a German general (probably Alfred Jodl) and Admiral von Friedeburg.

Celebrations took all forms. There was a huge bonfire on the 'Motte' of Bruce's Castle in Lochmaben and the Dumfries Standard reported that on VE Day, "Children were entertained to a cinema performance on Tuesday afternoon and on Wednesday they had sports… Flags and bunting gaily bedecked the shops and houses." On the next 2 pages are the children in Lochmaben Town Hall having fun at their first Christmas party after the war and a photograph of Lockerbie Primary School.

Amongst the party are:- Paul Roxburgh, Asher Banks, Jean Beck, John Ross, Frankie Wilson, Derek Moffat, Jeff Stone, Irene Bathgate,
Dorothy Ronnie, Sheila Beattie, Florence Brown, Douglas Bell, Sheila Richardson, Ida McColl, Tommy Duff, Joan Burns, Olive Lamb,
Ernie Richardson, May Green, Ernie Ferguson, Scott Paul, Johnnie Harkness, Ella Edgar, Nancy Brown, Jean Sloan, Billy Beck, Jack Wilkin,
James Grierson, Cathy Thomas, Thea Marrs, Margaret Barr (evacuee), Mick Duff, Jim Duff, Muriel Irving, Cathleen Thorburn, Maureen Ronnie,
Bobby Carruthers, Alfie Marrs, Mary McMillan, Rita McMillan, George Eastwood, Flemma McMichael, Lou Crolla, Pat Crolla, Becky Irving,
Bobby Armstrong, Margaret Brown, Adi Grierson, Ernie Moffat, Jim Ferguson, Davie Bell, Robbie McKie, Nancy Callendar, Nancy Harkness,
Billy Brown, Audrey Thorburn, Wilma Irving, Betty Thorburn, - Rae, Miss Mary Brown, Mrs White (from Sanatorium), Mrs Sloan (Hunterhouse),
Mrs Annie Beck, Mrs Adamson, Mrs McColl and Santa Claus who was possibly a Mr Barrons from the Sanatorium.

Some members of the Black Watch performing Highland dancing in McJerrow Park, Lockerbie as part of the general festivities of V J Day

P5 class of Lockerbie Primary children immediately after the war had ended. Most of them look quite happy!
Back row left to right: Jackie Swan, Robert McAdam, Alec Paterson, Kenneth McKenzie, 5, John Beattie, Martin Oliver, Tom Corrie, 9, 4th row John Dickson, Douglas Roxburgh, Bob Gracie, Jim Kelly, Tony Murray, Willie Linton, Charlie Johnstone, George McKinnon, Jack Gray, Maxwell Kerr - 3rd row Mary Mason, Suzanne Mollison, Margaret Carruthers, Betty Adamson, Kathleen Morton, Jean Notman, Mary Johnstone, 8, Phyllis Hunter,10, Esther Anderson - 2nd row Olive Cannon, Olive Broatch, Isobel Kerr, Mary Starkey, Shirley Murray, Pamela Robertson, Primrose Grieve, Elizabeth Smith, Eileen Hood, Janet Templeton, 11
Front row - Bill Muir, Roy Bell, John Moffat, Doreen Jamieson, Ian Jackson, Bert Waugh, Willlie Nicol.

Soldier returning home to his family and his newly built 'prefab' home in Moffat

Sadly many men and some women never came home. The war memorials which had been erected in the 1920s to remember the fallen of WW1 – the war that was to end all wars – were not always big enough to add the names of those who died during WW2. The WW2 memorial in Lockerbie is a plaque to be found upstairs in the Town Hall. In appendix 4 I have listed the names of the fallen from a few of the Annandale parishes.

Annandale had seen thousands of men, women and children arrive and leave in those six years, however several did remain, most because they got married here. Some partners would never have met, but for the war. The last POW camps had not been vacated until 1948, but however a new wave of visitors had come in 1947. The Ukranians who sought refuge from further terror were welcomed and integrated into Annandale society. Hallmuir Camp near Lockerbie was their refuge for some time until they found new homes and the Chapel built by them is still in existence.

Let's hope that the people of Annandale continue to extend a welcome to folk from all countries, especially in times of need, as they did so well in wartime.

Geoffrey, a friend of my Aunt was stationed in Annandale. He was from Leek in Staffordshire, but sadly he was one of the many who lost their lives on D-Day.

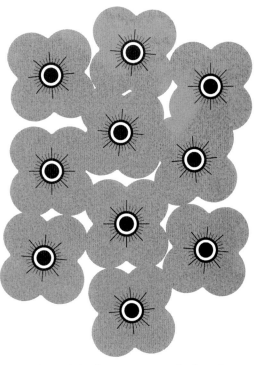

with permission from www.poppyscotland.org.uk

APPENDIX 1
WORLD WAR TWO TIMELINE (SELECTED EVENTS)

With thanks to Wikipedia for most of the following details.

Several key events of World War Two touched the lives of the contributors to this book.

1st Sept 1939 Operation Pied Piper- the evacuation of children from cities and ports to the countryside

3rd Sept 1939 Declaration of War on Germany

10th May 1940 Winston Churchill takes over from Neville Chamberlain as PM

26th May – 4th June 1940 Evacuation of Dunkirk

The Germans reached the coast on 20 May, separating the British Expeditionary Force (BEF) near Armentieres, the French First Army, and the Belgian Army further to the north from the majority of French troops south of the German lines. After reaching the Channel, the Germans swung north along the coast, threatening to capture the ports and trap the British and French forces before they could evacuate to Britain.

A total of five nations took part in the evacuation from Dunkirk - Britain, France, Belgium, the Netherlands and Poland.

10th June 1940 Italy declares war on Britain and France

July to October 1940 The Battle of Britain

September 1940 to May 1941 Blitz bombing of Clydebank, Greenock, London and other targets

May 1941 Rudolf Hess lands in Scotland

22nd June 1941 Operation Barbarossa - Germany invades Soviet Union

7th December 1941 Japan attacks Pearl Harbour (US naval base). Leads to US and Allies declaration of war on Japan.

Dec 1941 Japan invades Burma

15th Feb 1942 Fall of Singapore

July and October 1942 Battles of El Alamein At the First Battle, the advance of Axis (Italy and Nazi Germany) troops on Alexandria was blunted by the Allies, when the German Panzers tried to outflank the allied position.

At the Second Battle, allied forces broke the Axis line and forced them all the way back to Tunisia. Churchill said of this victory: "This is not the end, nor is it even the beginning of the end, but it is, perhaps, the end of the beginning." He also wrote, "Before Alamein, we had no victory and after it we had no defeats".

August 1942 Operation Pedestal was the final effort to supply Malta before she was forced to surrender.

14 merchant ships: **Almeria Lykes, Brisbane Star, Clan Ferguson, Decaulion, Empire Hope, Dorset, Glenorchy, Melbourne Star, Ohio, Port Chalmers, Rochester Castle, Santa Elisa, Waimarama, Wairangi**	9 Merchant ships sunk 3 damaged 5 arrive in Malta
2 battleships: **Nelson, Rodney**	Turned back as planned
4 aircraft carriers: **Victorious, Indomitable, Eagle, Furious**	1 aircraft carrier sunk, 1 damaged, 1 turns back as planned
7 cruisers: **Phoebe, Sirius, Charybdis, Nigeria, Kenya, Manchester, Cairo**	2 cruisers sunk, 2 turned back as planned
33 destroyers	1 destroyer sunk, 4 damaged
2 tugs, 4 corvettes, 4 minesweepers and 7 motor launches from Malta	

9th July 1943 The Allied invasion of Sicily, codenamed **Operation Husky**, was when the Allies took Sicily from the Axis. It was a large scale amphibious and airborne operation, followed by six weeks of land combat. The Allies drove Axis air and naval forces from the island; the Mediterranean's sea lanes were opened and Italian dictator Benito Mussolini was toppled from power. It opened the way to the invasion of Italy.

3rd September 1943 The Allied invasion of Italy was the allied landing on mainland Italy by the British Eighth Army. The main invasion force landed around Salerno on the western coast in **Operation Avalanche**.

Sept 1943 Italian Armistice

13th October 1943 Italy declares war on Germany

14th April 1944 The Bombay Explosion happened in the Victoria Dock of Bombay (now Mumbai) when the SS Fort Stikine carrying a mixed cargo of cotton bales, gold, ammunition including around 1,400 tons of explosives, caught fire and was destroyed in two giant blasts, scattering debris, sinking surrounding ships and killing at least 800 people.

6th June 1944 The Normandy Landings were also known as **Operation Neptune** and **Operation Overlord**. The landings commenced on Tuesday, June 6, 1944 (**D-Day**), beginning at 6:30 am. The assault was conducted in two phases: an air assault landing of American, British and Canadian troops shortly after midnight, and an amphibious landing of allied infantry and armoured divisions on the coast of France commencing at 6:30. The operation was the largest single day amphibious invasion of all time, with 160,000 troops landing on June 6. 195,7000 allied naval and merchant navy personnel in over 5,000 ships were involved. The landings took place along a 50mile (80 km) stretch of the coast divided into five sectors: Utah, Omaha, Gold, Juno and Sword.

17-25 September 1944 Operation Market Garden was an allied military operation, fought in the Netherlands and Germany. It was the largest airborne operation of all time.

It made large-scale use of airborne forces whose objectives were to secure a series of bridges over the main rivers of the German occupied Netherlands to allow a rapid advance by armoured units from the Dutch - Belgian border into northern Germany, across the Maas and two arms of the Rhine. This was intended to outflank the Siegfried Line and make possible an encirclement of the Ruhr area, Germany's industrial heartland.

The operation was initially successful with the capture of the Waal bridge at Nijmegen on September 20, but it was a failure overall since the planned Allied advance across the Rhine at Arnhem had to be abandoned. The British 1st Airborne Division did not secure the bridge at Arnhem, and although they managed to hold out near the bridge far longer than planned, the British XXX Corp failed to relieve them. The Rhine remained a barrier to the Allied advance for six additional months, until the offensives at Remagen, Oppenheim. Rees and Wesel in March 1945.

13-15th February 1945 The Bombing of Dresden by the British Royal Air Force(RAF) and United States Air Force (USAAF) twelve weeks before the surrender of the German armed forces. In four raids, 1,300 heavy bombers dropped more than 3,900 tons of high-explosive bombs on the city, the capital of the German state of Saxony. The resulting firestorm destroyed 13 square miles (34 km2) of the city centre. Estimates of civilian casualties vary greatly, but recent publications place the figure between 24,000 and 40,000.

7th May 1945 The German Surrender at Rheims ended the war in Europe. It was signed by representatives of the Oberkommando der Wehrmacht, the Allied Expeditionary Force and Soviet High Command. The date is known in the West as Victory in Europe Day.

(Wikipedia)

15th August 1945 VJ Day

The War against Japan ended after the two atomic bombs were dropped on Hiroshima and Nagasaki. The Japanese capitulated officially on 15th August 1945.

APPENDIX 2
IAN HENDERSON'S LOG

1.   26. 9.44   –   Calais. Day.

2.   28. 9.44   –   Calais. Day.

3.   6.10.44   –   Saarbrucken. Near collision.

4.   7.10.44   –   Emmerich. Day. Fullard shot down.

5.   14.10.44   –   Duisburg. Day.

6.   19.10.44   –   Stuttgart. Day. Attacked by ME 110. 7 hours.

7.   23.10.44   –   Essen. Night. Severe icing and thunder storms.

8.   25.10.44   –   Essen. Day. Hit 4 times.

9.   28.10.44   –   Cologne. Night. Temp. minus 40c. Almost struck by bombs
                                                    from above.

10.   30.10.44   –   Cologne. Night. Landed at Dunholme Lodge by mistake.

11.   11.11.44   –   Wanne Eikel. Night. Temp. minus 40c.

12.   16.11.44   –   Duren. Day.

13.   18.11.44   –   Wanne Eikel. Night. Diverted.

14.   29.11.44   –   Dortmund. Day. X-ray missing.

15.   3.12.44   –   Urft Dam. Day. Caught fire and landed at Brussels.

16.   28.12.44   –   Bonn. Night.

17.   5. 1.45   –   Royan. Night.

18.   28. 1.45   –   Stuttgart. Night. Jones missing (shot down).

19.   3. 2.45   –   Bottrop. Night. Freeborne missing.

20.   4. 2.45   –   Heligoland. Night. Mine laying. Crane in S. Sugar shot up
                                                    badly.

21.   8. 2.45   –   Politz. Night. 9 hours. Hit in port engine.

22.   13. 2.45   –   Dresden. Night. 10½ hours.

23.   14. 2.45   –   Chemnitz. Night. Hit 5 times - once in port tailplane.

24.   21. 2.45   –   Duisberg. Night. Saw 5 aircraft go down in flames.

25.   1. 3.45   –   Mannheim. Day. Rhodes in U Uncle blew up over The Wash.

26.   5. 3.45   –   Chemnitz. Night. Saw 4 aircraft go down in flames.
                                                    Weather bad.

27.   15. 3.45   –   Misburg (Hanover). Night. Near collision.

28.   21. 3.45   –   Bremen. Day. Hit 3 times on port tailplane, fusilage and
                                                    starboard wing.

29.   24. 3.45   –   Largendreen. Day. Hit 4 times.

30.   27. 3.45   –   Paderborne. Day. Near collision.

31.   4. 4.45   –   Lutzbendorf. Night. Near collision. Hit once.

Appendix 3
Food Rationing

Food Rationing

Foods were gradually rationed. In January1940 the first foods rationed were bacon, ham, sugar and butter.

In March, meat was rationed
In July, tea, margarine, cooking fat and cheese
March 1941, jam, marmalade, treacle and syrup oil
June 1941, distribution of eggs controlled
Nov 1941, milk controlled
July 1942, sweets were rationed.

Basic rations varied at times, but normally were:
50g cheese
50g butter
100g margarine
100g cooking fat
3pints milk
225g sugar
450g preserves every 2 months
1 egg
50g tea
350 g sweets every 4 weeks

Dried milk and dried eggs became available after 1941. Vegetarians surrendered their meat coupons and received more cheese.

APPENDIX 4
WAR MEMORIALS

I have noted the names of the fallen of World War Two from a small selection of Memorials in Annandale.

Annan

Royal Navy
J Bell
WC Cuthbertson
ADH Elder
JT Kerr
T Lawson
J Thomson
JS Woodman
Merchant Seamen
RG Bell
WS Brown
CH Crompton
Royal Marines
H Currie
Green Howards
AT Semple
RAF
GE Butler
JS Flockhart
W Fleming
WT Holliday
JJ Leitch
CR Robinson
J Scaife
H Taylor
R Wilkin
DL Willacy
Scots Guards
W Linn
Royal Scots
J Irving
W Robertson
RAC
W Pool
S Thomson

RE
D Tinning

Annan

JB Tyson
RCOS
JJ Adamson
RASC W Brydson
RAOC D Anderson
RTC WS Lupton
RA
J Smith
MA Wiliiamson
W Campbell
JJ Carroll
R Davie
WS Elliot
R Fox
A Gillies
WJ Grierson
WJT Irving
TG Little
KOSB
JT Beattie
J Dalgleish
AS Grierson
TR Halbert
J Notman
A Schoolar
RT Scott
JC Semple
Royal Inn Fus
RJ Grierson
Seaf Highrs
BR Fairbairn
SA Johnstone
Gord Highrs A Scott
Came Highrs J Crombie

Also in Annan there is a memorial footbridge across the river. "In memory of Surgeon Lt. William Graham Cuthbertson RNVR and the men and women of the burgh and parish of Annan who gave their lives during the 1939-45 war."

Applegarth and Sibbaldbie (in the church)
L'Cpl George Arnott S.High.
GDMN. William John Richardson S.G.
Gun. Gladstone Scott R.A.
Ab. James Waugh R.N.

Brydekirk
Signalman JJ Adamson RCS
Pte TR Halbert KOSB
AC2 WC Johnston RAF
Trooper CA Rafferty RTR
LAC J Wallace RAF
PO WCT Welsh RN

Cummertrees
Samuel Crawford
J Irving Dalgleish
Alexander J Hyslop
James Miller
Christian C Norgaard
John Ramage

Dornock
James Burnett
Kenneth C Comrie
Leslie C Comrie
Robert CP Carmont
James Cowan
William Conchie
Thomas Dalton
John Heslop
William JT Irving
Robert Maxwell
Jack E Phillips
Harry Pitt
David S Scott
John Shannon
Arthur JH Shields
David W Smith
Robert Vallance
James Warwick

Dornock

Dalton

Dalton
Pte AH Carruthers VDF Malaya
Pte James SM Dunn Gordons
Pte John Halliday KOSB
Major G Scott- Nicholson Lanarkshire Yeomanry
BDR Thomas Watret RA

Memorial in Dryfesdale Church

Dryfesdale (In Town Hall)

George Adamson	John A Grierson
William Bell	Peter D Johnstone
Robert Black	Charles WP Lawson
James Burgess	John Andrew Martin
W Watson Callender	William Nicol
William Cannon	Isabella Oliver
Duncan B Cooper	John B Richardson
William J Currie	William Scott
John Meikle Dymock	Ian H Sinclair
Walter R Fletcher	William Tait
John S Flockhart	David Wightman
William Fyfe	**And in Dryfesdale Church**
George TW Gibson	Doctor MD Winning (Burma
James Edward Graham	1942)

Johnstone

Johnstone

J. S. Dundas, KOSB
R. R. Houston, ACS
P. Murray, Merchant Navy
C. Simpson, East Yorks

Lochmaben

Lochmaben

Pte D Arnold KOSB
L Cpl A Blackstock Black Watch
Pte J Carruthers KOSB
Sgt JT Cockburn RAFVR
L Bdr WR Cameron RA
Sgt DJ Green RAF
Sgt J Holmes RAF
Drv WLR Hunter RASC
Sgt J Halifax RA
AC 2S K Little RAF
Pte Robertina Murray ATS
LAC/W Jessie Richardson WAAF
Pte TA Robertson KOSB
Lieut JKW Sloan Grenadier Guards
Pte A Smith Royal Scots
Sgt. D Turnbull RAF
ABM Wilson RN

In addition in Lochmaben cemetery the following men are commemorated:

Private JA Gelston McQueen Home Guard
Sergeant Andrew Taylor Gibson Pioneer Corps
Private Gordon Miller Henderson Royal Scots.

Middlebie (inside church)

L/Cpl James John Jardine Scots Guards
Able Seaman Robert Wm. Johnstone Royal Navy
L/Sgt Thomas Wilson Black Watch
L/Cpl Alexander Allan Lockerbie Royal Scots Fusiliers

Moffat

Nethermill

Pte JB Bell Black Watch
Serg, Roderick Campbell RAFVR
AC/1 JJ Douglas RAF
P/O CH Hannan RAFVR
Fus Adam McFadzean RSF
Pte Alex, FTMcNeish RASC
Pte John Muirhead KOSB
P/O Jas, L Shiells DFM RAFVR

Ruthwell

FT/Sgt George R Irving RAF
Pte William McWhirter KOSB

Moffat

F/LT AT Hope Robertson RAF
Lt Col CJW Simpson Mahratta LI
F/Sgt WD Smail RAF
Pte DL Stewart Seaforths
Sgt JT Corbett RAF
Sgt P Dicerbo RAF
Pte J Donaldson Hampshire Regt
Dvr S Ferguson RE
Lt I G Gow Scots Guards
Pte SA Little KOSB
Capt AD Mitchell Royal Scots
Cpl WC Rae Blackwatch
Sgt JS Beattie RAF
Pte WH Bell KOSB
Lt OW Butler RAC
Pte H Corbett RSF

Nethermill

APPENDIX 5
BIBLIOGRAPHY

Individuals' interviews and stories

Information from:-

The Annandale Herald and Record Newspapers 1939-45

Dumfries and Galloway Standard and Advertiser newspapers 1945, 1999

"The Home Guard Historical Record 1940-44 1st (Dumfriesshire) Battalion", Lieut.- Col. Ralph Hope- Vere (Dec 1944 Herald Press, Lockerbie)

Lochmaben Town Council minutes

Woman magazine 1942 (National Library of Scotland) HJ9.1220

Log Books of Johnstonebridge Primary School

Admission records of Lockerbie Academy

WW2 Display folder by Lockerbie British Legion (Lockerbie Library)

"Alfred the Great", Maria Bojanitz

"Temporary Settlements and Transient Populations- The Legacy of Britain's Prisoner of War Camps: 1940-1948", Professor J Anthony Hellen

"Memories of Moffat", Emilio Dicerbo

"The Beach Commandos", A Cecil Hampshire, pub 1983 William Kimber and Co Ltd, London

"Land at war 1945" from the War Facsimilies pub. Stationery Office Norwich

List of aircraft crashes - Ewart Library, DG(358.4)

Archives from the Barony Agricultural College Library

Internet:-Wikipedia; websites:-
www.ww2propaganda.org
www.wartimememories.co.uk
http://slvtv.southlanarkshire.tv/
www.st-andrews.ac.uk/~pv/pv/courses/posters/index//html

Photographs and illustrations are author's own; borrowed from interviewees; photographed articles from The Annandale Herald and Record Newspapers, 1940-45; from Wikipedia; and websites:-
www.powtaiwan.org
www.poppyscotland.org.uk
www.caringonthehomefront.org.uk